T0376057

Corporate Social Responsibility and Civil Society in India

Nandini Deo

ANTHEM PRESS

Anthem Press
An imprint of Wimbledon Publishing Company
www.anthempress.com

This edition first published in UK and USA 2024
by ANTHEM PRESS
75–76 Blackfriars Road, London SE1 8HA, UK
or PO Box 9779, London SW19 7ZG, UK
and
244 Madison Ave #116, New York, NY 10016, USA

© Nandini Deo 2024

The author asserts the moral right to be identified as the author of this work.

All rights reserved. Without limiting the rights under copyright reserved above,
no part of this publication may be reproduced, stored or introduced into
a retrieval system, or transmitted, in any form or by any means
(electronic, mechanical, photocopying, recording or otherwise),
without the prior written permission of both the copyright
owner and the above publisher of this book.

British Library Cataloguing-in-Publication Data
A catalogue record for this book is available from the British Library.

Library of Congress Cataloging-in-Publication Data
A catalog record for this book has been requested.
2024935713

ISBN-13: 978-1-83998-596-6 (Hbk)
ISBN-10: 1-83998-596-8 (Hbk)

Cover image credit: Deepak Amembal
https://magictravels.blogspot.com/

This title is also available as an e-book.

CONTENTS

Acknowledgments	v
Introduction: Corporate Social Responsibility and Civil Society in India	1
1. Corporations and Civil Society Organizations	21
2. The Matchmaker State	41
3. Inclusive and Sustainable Development	67
4. Corporate Promise and Reality	91
5. Civil Society Responses	115
6. After Corporate Social Responsibility	133
Index	145

ACKNOWLEDGMENTS

My thanks go out to the many people who made this study possible, but who don't share the fault for its shortcomings. Lehigh University provided the funding, research assistants, and brilliant colleagues without whom I could not have conducted the fieldwork or made sense of my field notes. Din Ambar, Breena Holland, Janet Laible, Al Wurth, Ziad Munson, Terry-Ann Jones, Terri Clemens, Amardeep Singh, Khurram Hussain, Lisa Getzler, Brian Fife, and Bill Bulman asked helpful questions and supported me in small and big ways. The students in my courses on South Asian Politics and Social Entrepreneurship heard my ideas and evaluated evidence with me before it was digested into a coherent story. Thank you for experimenting with me. My Iaccoca interns and Creative Inquiry team helped with gathering data and organizing ideas. Miko Goliati helped with the news archive and did a site visit of his own. Your curiosity and energy sustained me when I was flagging.

In India, I am grateful to Manjeet Kripalani and Neelam Deo for sharing the network of Gateway House and the incredible team there—from Akhsay, to Purvaja, to Blaise, to Celine, to Samir, and everyone who was so warm and welcoming. Shyam Vyas helped with all kinds of arrangements over the years for which I am grateful. Sujata, Pallavi Upendra, Dhanushree, and Praful took wonderful care of me and the kids on our trips to India. Pushpa Sundar, Neera Chandhoke, Sumita Pahwa, Sarbeswar Sahoo, Margit van Wessel, Rajeshwari Balasubramanian, Rita Manchanda, Suparna Katyani, Farhat Naz, Reetika Syal, Yogesh Mishra, Nandini Sundar, Manisha Madhava, Varsha Ainapure, and Bhaskar Chatterjee shared their time and attention with generosity. Rajitha Gopinath, Poorva Abhishek, Pinky Kothari, and the brilliant kids at Sadhana Learning Center distracted me and also gave me space to write in their library. Rushab is a true visionary in bringing democracy to work and Pankaj is the best advisor—always questioning.

My parents remain steadfast in their support—offering introductions, corrections, and their company at every turn. Kavi and Asha were born while I was working on this book. They are the best kind of speed bumps. Gyan was already with me and has tolerated my interest in politics his whole life. Tim is the partner who makes it all possible—our family and my work. I can't thank you enough.

Introduction

CORPORATE SOCIAL RESPONSIBILITY AND CIVIL SOCIETY IN INDIA

India's wealthiest individual, Mukesh Ambani, has a net worth of $51,400,000,000. In response to the COVID-19 pandemic, he donated $67,000,000 to national relief efforts.[1] Does this strike you as a commendable act of generosity and benevolence? Or does it seem like a woefully inadequate gesture designed to deflect criticism of the man for his obscene wealth in the face of starving millions? Corporate social responsibility (CSR) and billionaire philanthropy are like a Rorschach test—the same act can look very different depending on how we understand its intentions and its consequences. In this book, I examine the politics of CSR in India to assess its ability to advance inclusive and sustainable development. One need not begin with a particular commitment to expanding or eliminating the practice of CSR. Rather, the focus is on how CSR is remaking the practices and agendas of civic organizations that are being encouraged to collaborate with business to advance equality and prosperity.

Civil society organizations (CSOs) and corporations have a history of hostility to each other. According to CSO workers, businesses selfishly exploit workers, despoil natural resources, and distort democracy to serve their own profit-making ends. According to business executives, NGOs are hopelessly naïve, inefficient, and interfere in the market in ways that reduce economic growth. And yet, in the past decade, more and more NGOs and businesses are collaborating in new ways. Individuals from both sectors are setting up social impact enterprises and social investing funds are increasing. The more traditional forms of corporate–CSO collaboration have expanded as more funds are flowing from business to the social sector. The divide between the corporate sector and civil society seems to be narrowing. Why is this happening and what are its consequences? This book

---

1 Raghunathan, Anu. 2020. "Indian donations soar as covid-19 pandemic widens" April 2. *Forbes.*

2   CORPORATE SOCIAL RESPONSIBILITY AND CIVIL SOCIETY

examines these trends in India, where since 2013, the state has mandated co-operation between the largest firms and CSOs in pursuit of inclusive and sustainable development.

Believers in CSR cheer the creation of new collaborations and programs like Akshaya Patra which provides mid-day meals in schools and is largely funded by corporations. They argue that doing good and doing well are compatible goals that should be more widely imitated.[2] Skeptics or Nihilists view such innovations as a means for greedy corporations to whitewash their misdeeds through a performance of charity.[3] Of course, some Nihilists have a neoliberal view of corporations in which their pursuit of their own narrow self-interest is actually their highest good and greatest contribution to society. Based on interviews with policymakers, CSO workers, corporate executives, and researchers who are assessing CSR interventions I show how corporate jargon and money are remaking the social sector. My students and I interviewed 56 corporations about their CSR activities and almost 100 CSOs. In addition to interviews, I draw upon the gray literature created by CSOs and corporations describing their programs and their vision for social service through their websites, journals, blogs, and annual reports. The changes in the social sector are making it harder to solve the pressing problems of poverty, inequality, and social marginalization. This book offers evidence that CSR is unlikely to contribute to inclusive and sustainable development. By claiming to be "helpers" corporations can silence their critics and thus avoid making the deeper shifts in business models needed in order to create a more just and sustainable society.

Mismatch: a Personal Experience

In the Fall of 2018, I met Khanjan Mehta for a coffee. He is the founding Director for Creative Inquiry at Lehigh University, an engineer, and a Mumbaikar like me. I was curious to learn more about what he was trying to create at Lehigh University. He explained that he was looking for faculty

---

2 Acharya, Nish. 2017. "India's CSR: Taking Singles instead of hitting Sixes" Equal Innovation Feb 10 Available at https://www.linkedin.com/pulse/indias-csr-taking-singles-instead-hitting-sixes-acharya (accessed April 25, 2020); Chatterjee, B., and N. Mitra. 2017. "CSR Should Contribute to the National Agenda in Emerging Economies—the 'Chatterjee Model'." *International Journal of Corporate Social Responsibility*. 2(1). https://doi.org/10.1186/s40991-017-0012-1 (accessed April 25, 2020).

3 Roy, Arundhati. 2014. *Capitalism: A Ghost Story*. Verso: New York, NY; Giridharadas, Anand. 2108. *Winners Take All: The Elite Charade of Changing the World*. Knopf: New York, NY.

INTRODUCTION

with a research agenda that could involve undergraduate students who would be trained jointly by the faculty member and his team to think about how to find creative solutions to real-world problems. He had taken students to Southeast Asia and Africa to introduce commercial mushroom farming, to build micro greenhouses, and he was eager to find more projects in the social and humanistic fields. Khanjan drinks a lot of coffee and talks very fast with great enthusiasm about the deep learning that happens outside of the classroom in collaborative and motivated teams. It is easy to get swept up in his excitement about what is possible when faculty and students work together on high impact projects.

He asked me about my research and I told him how this CSR project had already involved students who came to India with me in 2015 to interview corporate representatives about their CSR programs. We had interviewed 56 business leaders, collected data on another 150, and shared our findings via blog posts hosted by a think tank called Gateway House in Mumbai. Khanjan thought this was wonderful, I was wonderful, and the students were wonderful. We were out there getting answers to policy questions, solving problems, and making a positive impact on the world.

By the end of the meeting, I had agreed to essentially teach a mini-course, mentoring five undergraduate students with the goal of taking them to Mumbai with me to conduct more interviews and perhaps make a documentary film and write conference papers with a view to having publications based on our work. This is a hugely ambitious task in the social sciences- a typical empirical paper with five coauthors takes about 2–3 years to conceive and submit for publication. I was not going to be paid anything for this work. Instead, my own research enthusiasm and desire to teach students research skills was to be my chief compensation. I would be given a small research budget and my flight to India would be paid for. Khanjan's office would create a shortlist of student candidates for me to select from and I would help those students prepare for presentations they would be doing in the weekly seminar he runs.

Monica, Fernando, Erin, Riya, and Poppy[4] were smart, ambitious, and eager to start making an impact on the world. As we began our weekly meetings, I wanted to encourage their enthusiasm but also needed to explain that we were not going to be changing the world. Our aim was to identify knowledge gaps, conduct research, and hopefully share some policy or process improvements with the businesses, civil society organizations, and bureaucrats involved in CSR in India. Perhaps the Indian case would teach us something we could offer to other countries as a model for how to (or

---

4 Student names are pseudonyms to protect their privacy.

4   CORPORATE SOCIAL RESPONSIBILITY AND CIVIL SOCIETY

how not to) create a healthy CSR ecosystem. All of this would take years of listening to the actors on the ground, looking for patterns, analyzing data, asking questions, and eventually synthesizing it into a narrative that makes some sense. Despite this timeline, we were on the clock to get enough done in the Spring semester that they would be ready for fieldwork in India over the summer and then we would keep working together in the Fall.

The students ranged from first to fourth years, with a range of majors, and only one had any previous exposure to India as a heritage student. We began with an introduction to Indian history, politics, and culture. Then I spent some time teaching them about the CSR law and how businesses were responding to it. I tasked them with finding and analyzing some of the academic and gray literature on CSR in India. Meanwhile, they were also hearing from Khanjan who was urging them to think big and zero in on the impact they would have on CSR in India. By the end of the semester when the students had to present their project to a panel of academics and industry people, they were quite discouraged. The feedback they received made it clear that their project was not one that would lead to an innovative product or process that would help CSR practitioners in India which is what their fellowship was orienting them toward. They also felt like I related to them as my research assistants— asking them to read and summarize, rather than as collaborators whose own analysis was valued. One student who left the program at this point offered some very candid and clear feedback. Essentially, Khanjan and my vision for the team were at odds. He wanted them to create something tangible that could help people right away. I wanted them to understand the context and learn how to see things from the perspective of the people involved.

The differences in outcome that we expected, the disparate timelines, and the opposite intuitions about what matters and what is not significant in the field held by their two mentors made it impossible for the students to either accomplish what they wanted or to feel as if their contributions were valued. Despite this, four of them were supposed to accompany me to India that summer. Meanwhile, I was heading to India for the Fall semester on a research leave and was distracted by my own preparations for this field visit. As Khanjan's office worked on the logistics of the students' travel, I was asked to sign a form stating that in the event of an emergency, I would prioritize the university students' safety over that of my own preschool-aged children. I could not in good faith sign such a document and refused. At that point, the risk assessment team at the university decided I could not be the sole faculty member accompanying the students on this research visit. When I pointed out how such a policy would disproportionately affect young mothers I was met with some murmurs of sympathy but otherwise dismissed. An educational support organization was brought on board to provide the supervision of

INTRODUCTION 5

health and safety for the students and I was to only worry about directing their research. As this was being worked out another student found that her anticipated costs for the summer internship she was completing before meeting us in India made it impossible for her to join us. So now we were down to three students and myself. Then, a third student withdrew as the details of the trip kept changing, especially the financial aspects of it. With only two students left, Khanjan made the difficult call to cancel the trip.

As the fieldwork and the fellowship structure crumbled, I reflected on the ways in which this attempt at bringing the design thinking and entrepreneurial spirit of a world of product creation and marketing was colliding with a world of ethnographic habits of close listening and immersion in local context. I came to realize that it actually encapsulates perfectly much of what I kept seeing in my research on CSR in India. The very impulses that made my collaboration with Khanjan work so poorly were some of the very same dynamics causing CSR partnerships to fail to create the inclusive and sustainable development outcomes they promised. Since then, I have had other successful collaborations with Khanjan and his office. I think we are both trying to be much more explicit at the outset about our expectations and boundaries. So, although I do think it is difficult to collaborate across the corporate-civil society divide in the larger world of CSR, personally I am not giving up on it.

Corporations and Civil Society in India

In this book, I describe the hopes for CSR in India, how the policies were designed, and why they never quite work as they should. This book engages three sets of scholarly and policy debates. The broadest literature that frames this book is the literature on inclusive and sustainable development. Development economists such as Jeffrey Sachs, C. K. Prahlad, Acemoglu, and Robinson suggest that greater investment in the rule of law combined with greater freedom for business will lead to prosperity.[5] Critics such as Ferguson, Escobar, Grown, and Sen suggest that this approach is flawed because it underestimates the stickiness of power in shaping the status quo. These critics point to the role of technocratic expertise in depoliticizing poverty,[6] the role

---

5 Sachs, J. 2005. *The End of Poverty; How We Can Make It Happen in Our Lifetime*. New York City, NY: Penguin; Prahalad, C. K. 2005. *The Fortune at the Bottom of the Pyramid—Eradicating Poverty through Profits*. Upper Saddle River, NJ: Wharton School Publishing; Acemoglu, D. and J. A. Robinson. 2012. *Why Nations Fail: The Origins of Power, Prosperity, and Poverty*. New York City, NY: Crown.
6 Ferguson, J. 1994. *The Anti-Politics Machine*. Stanford, CA: Stanford University Press.

6   CORPORATE SOCIAL RESPONSIBILITY AND CIVIL SOCIETY

of international systems in maintaining global inequality[7] and the exclusion of marginalized voices in policymaking.[8] I advance this literature by making explicit the politics of collaboration in CSR development initiatives. When we see how poverty is produced and actively maintained, it is harder to be sanguine about elite-driven attempts to alleviate it.

Second, there is a lively public debate about the role of business in advancing development. As mentioned above, Roy and Giridharadas have argued that CSR and billionaire philanthropy actually exacerbate problems of poverty and inequality.[9] In addition, scholars such as McGoey and Kohl-Arenas offer in-depth critiques of particular foundations and development initiatives sponsored by big business.[10] But, Jenkins shows that many development agencies—bilateral and multilateral, have adopted a much more positive view on CSR.[11] The embrace by government and corporations of this mission to help through CSR is documented in a hundred mission and vision statements in annual reports. This book contributes to this policy debate by trying to identify the conditions under which CSR can help or hurt inclusive development.

A third area of relevant scholarship is the literature on the professionalization of NGOs which is particularly advanced in reference to civil society organizations working for women's rights. In the 1990s, Alvarez described the NGOization of women's advocacy organizations in Latin America. Since then Karim has shown how development CSOs can function as "shadow states" as their power and influence grow. Seuty Sabar and Srila Roy explore the consequences of greater professionalization of women's organizations

---

7   Escobar, A. 1994. *Encountering Development*. Princeton, NJ: Princeton University Press; Easterly, W. 2006. *White Man's Burden*. New York City, NY: Penguin.

8   Grown, C. and Sen, G. 1985. *Development Crises and Alternative Visions: Third World Women's Perspectives*. New York City, NY: Monthly Review Press; van Wessel, M., N. Deo, R. Manchanda, S. Sahoo, B. Rajeshwari, S. Katyaini, R. Syal, F. Naz, and Y. Mishra. 2019. *Starting from the South: Advancing Southern Leadership in Civil Society Advocacy Collaborations*. Policy Brief. *Include Platform*. Available at https://includeplatform.net/wp-content/uploads/2019/12/Policy-brief-1-Starting-from-the-South.pdf (accessed May 4, 2020).

9   Roy, Arundhati. 2014. *Capitalism: A Ghost Story*. New York, NY: Verso; Giridharadas, Anand. 2108. *Winners Take All: The Elite Charade of Changing the World*. New York, NY: Knopf.

10 McGoey, L. 2015. *No Such Thing as a Free Gift*. New York City, NY: Verso Books; Kohl-Arenas, E. 2015. *The Self-Help Myth: How Philanthropy Fails to Alleviate Poverty*. Berkeley, CA: University of California Press.

11 Jenkins, R. 2005. "Globalization, Corporate Social Responsibility and Poverty." *International Affairs*, 81: 525–540.

INTRODUCTION

in South Asia.[12] They showed how the institutionalization of CSOs can deradicalize them but that it also allows non-elite women the possibility of employment in the social sector which in turn can make CSOs more responsive to grassroots needs. I advance these debates by showing that we are moving from the NGOization of civil society to a corporatization of civil society. This transformation has important implications for advocacy agendas and methods.

There are only a handful of books about CSR in India, and none that focus on collaborations with civil society. Some authors largely target business professionals to advise them on how to engage in CSR.[13] Pushpa Sundar frames this literature by describing the evolution and history of CSR as part of a larger history of philanthropy in South Asia.[14] Two, more analytical, books inform my thinking. The first offers a useful study of how Indian CSR differs from global norms and the second is the first book to theorize CSR in India from a sociological perspective.[15] *CSR and Civil Society* is distinctive in two ways: First, the focus on corporate–civil society collaborations is novel empirical terrain. Second, the book speaks to both academic and development policymaking audiences. Development practitioners and students of development politics may find this a useful text. And I hope this book will be useful to development studies, political economy, or South Asian politics students.

Before the 2013 law was passed, CSR was already being studied by scholars. The main thrust of their work was to understand why companies engaged in CSR and to assess its impact. Atul Sood and Bimal Arora offer a valuable overview of the historical development of CSR and a rich description of

---

12 Alvarez, Sonia E. 1999. "Advocating Feminism: The Latin American Feminist NGO 'Boom'," *International Feminist Journal of Politics*. 1(2), 181–209; Karim, Lamia. 2011. *Microfinance and its Discontents: Women in Debt in Bangladesh*. Minneapolis, MN: University of Minnesota Press; Sabar, Seuty. 2013. "Did 'NGOization' Deradicalize the Women's Movement?" Alal O Dulal Available at https://alalodulal.org/2013/05/28/ngoization/ (accessed May 4, 2020); Roy, Srila. 2012. New South Asian Feminisms London: Zed Books.

13 Agarwal, Sanjay. 2008. *Corporate Social Responsibility in India*. New Delhi: Sage; Lumde, Nirbhay. 2018. *Corporate Social Responsibility in India: A Practitioner's Perspective*. Chennai: Notion; Mitra, Nayan and Rene Schimpedeter (Eds.). 2017. *Corporate Social Responsibility in India: Cases and Developments after the Legal Mandate*. Geneva: Springer and 2020. *Mandated Corporate Social Responsibility: Evidence from India*. Geneva: Springer which offer a series of case studies of CSR projects in India.

14 Sundar, Pushpa. 2012. *Business and Community*. New Delhi: Sage.

15 Chakrabarty, Bidyut. 2011. *Corporate Social Responsibility in India*. London: Routledge; Krichewsky, Damien. 2019. *Corporate Social Responsibility and Economic Responsiveness in India*. Cambridge: Cambridge University Press.

8   CORPORATE SOCIAL RESPONSIBILITY AND CIVIL SOCIETY

the ways in which it is being carried out. They argue that Indian CSR is domestically driven, building on older traditions of charity and business family philanthropy. They also suggest that a greater role could be played by NGOs acting as watchdogs of corporate action in shaping the types of CSR companies adopted.[16] A decade later Majumdar and Saini, and Aggarwal and Jha argue that CSR in India was becoming more strategic and becoming more responsive to community demands.[17] Taking an interpretive approach, Dhanesh found that the immorality of inequality and the strategic long-term sustainability of the corporation itself were dominant frames in how business elites explained why they engage in CSR.[18] Some argue that Indian CSR should be understood using the lens of the sustainable development goals and the role that business can play in achieving those.[19] Others argue for a more capabilities centered approach to evaluating CSR.[20] All of these authors agreed that most of the work on theorizing CSR is based on the Global North and that there is a dearth of research on the Indian case. This book provides some of this empirical work and also offers a theoretical account of CSR based on the experience of an emerging economy. These insights should travel to other contexts as well.

Believers and Nihilists

To a large extent, the thinking around corporate engagement with civil society can be described as splitting along a "believer" and "nihilist" divide. Believers are cheerleaders for corporate involvement in the social sector, hyping the ways in which corporations and their business practices can solve seemingly intractable social problems. Ultimately they see corporations (and the people who work for them) as having good intentions which can lead to positive impact.

The brilliant researchers at McKinsey write passionately about the corporate role in sustainable and inclusive development. "How should

---

16 Sood, Atul and Bimal Arora. 2006. "A Review of Corporate Social Responsibility in India" United Nations Research Institute for Social Development November Vol 18.

17 Majumdar, Satyajit and Gordhan K. Saini. 2016. "CSR in India: Critical Review and Exploring Entrepreneurial Opportunities." *Journal of Entrepreneurship and Innovating in Emerging Economies.* 2(1), 56–79; Aggarwal, Vijita Singh and Aruna Jha. 2019. "Pressures of CSR in India: An Institutional Perspective." *Journal of Strategy and Management.* 12(2), 227–242.

18 Dhanesh, G. S. 2015. "Why Corporate Social Responsibility? An Analysis of Drivers of CSR in India." *Management Communication Quarterly.* 29(1), 114–129.

19 Bhatt, Sanjai and Lakshya Kadiyan. 2022. "Corporate Social Responsibility and Social Development in India: An Interface." *Social Development Issues.* 44(3), 23–37.

20 Renouard, Cecile and Cecile Ezvan. 2018. "Corporate Social Responsibility Towards Human Development: A Capabilities Framework." *Business Ethics.* 1(12), 1–12.

INTRODUCTION 9

the world confront its most pressing environmental and social challenges? An answer lies in sustainable, inclusive growth—that is, economic growth that provides the financial resources needed to contain climate change, promote natural capital and biodiversity, empower households, and promote equitable opportunity. Any effort to usher in such growth will need many stakeholders, but businesses, which drive more than 70 percent of global GDP, will be a key player."[21] They go on to provide a framework for businesses to identify four paths toward becoming impact players in creating globally sustainable and inclusive development. Implicit is the idea that businesses are doing the best they can to promote sustainability and inclusivity within constraints that they cannot resist individually. They conclude, "We hope that this research and framework will help companies do the important work of setting priorities and convening the right partnerships so that they can move swiftly from aspiration to action." That is, they assume that corporations have aspirations to do good in the world. This may be a strategic posture to be more persuasive. But it also reinforces the idea that business and growth are sacrosanct, with adjustments only needed on the edges of the global economy.

Another global consulting firm, KPMG describes the role of CSR in helping India achieve the targets articulated by the SDGs. They see collaboration by civil society and corporations as key to documenting success stories and extending innovations. "Private sector can bring a fresh perspective to the path set for achieving the SDGs [...] this collaborative public private effort is likely to make the journey relatively easy and achievable at an accelerated pace."[22] Not only can corporations contribute their financial resources to sustainable and inclusive development, they can also conduct research, design processes, and create more effective policies. In August 2019, the American Business Roundtable released a new understanding of the "Purpose of a Corporation" signed by over 200 CEOs of some of the world's largest companies. They said that, "While each of our individual companies serves its own corporate purpose, we share a fundamental commitment to all of our stakeholders."[23]

---

21 McKinsey and Company. 2022. "Toward a sustainable, inclusive, growing future: The role of business" https://www.mckinsey.com/featured-insights/sustainable-inclusive-growth/toward-a-sustainable-inclusive-growing-future-the-role-of-business?cid=eml-web (accessed November 2023).

22 KPMG. 2017. "Leveraging CSR to Achieve SDGs" Global Compact Network India. Available at https://opportunity.businessroundtable.org/opportunity/commitment (accessed November 2023).

23 Business Roundtable. 2019. "Statement on the Purpose of a Corporation' August 19. Available at https://system.businessroundtable.org/app/uploads/sites/5/2023/02/WSJ_BRT_POC_Ad.pdf (accessed September 2022).

CORPORATE SOCIAL RESPONSIBILITY AND CIVIL SOCIETY

That is, they moved from being responsible only to their shareholders to being responsible to shareholders, consumers, workers, community, and America. This shift is remarkable as it reflects a faith in corporations to be able to be responsible to all these stakeholders and to the belief that doing good will allow them to do well.

Scholars have offered empirical research to support CSR as a tool for better business. By better they mean both better for society and better for shareholders. "While it is valuable for a company to engage in CSR for altruistic and ethical justifications, the highly competitive business world in which we live requires that, in allocating resources to socially responsible initiatives, firms continue to consider their own business needs. In the last decade, in particular, empirical research has brought evidence of the measurable payoff of CSR initiatives on firms as well as their stakeholders."[24] Studies have shown that more diverse boards have higher profits.[25] Others have shown that corporations with greater commitment to ESG principles have greater success than those who do not try to be more sustainably oriented.[26] This is a controversial literature but what I am interested in is the fact that these arguments are being made at all. That is, to persuade corporations to do the right thing, scholars and others want to convince them they can do it without any pain or loss.

Even the United Nations takes an optimistic line on the role of corporations in achieving the sustainable development goals. "Business enterprises are a major source of investment, innovation, and development and can be a major driver in achieving the Sustainable Development Goals."[27] Speaking of global challenges, former secretary general Kofi Annan listed ambitious

---

24 Carroll, A. B. and K. M. Shabana. 2010. "The Business Case for Corporate Social Responsibility: A Review of Concepts, Research and Practice." *International Journal of Management Reviews.* 12, 85–105.

25 McKinsey and Company. 2020. "Diversity Wins: How Inclusion Matters" Available at https://www.mckinsey.com/featured-insights/diversity-and-inclusion/diversity-wins-how-inclusion-matters#/ (accessed May 6, 2024).

26 Aydoğmuş, Mahmut, Güzhan Gülay, and Korkmaz Ergun. 2022. "Impact of ESG Performance on Firm Value and Profitability." *Borsa Istanbul Review.* 22(2), S119–S127. For a contrary view see Cerciello, M., F. Busato, and S. Taddeo. 2023. "The Effect of Sustainable Business Practices on Profitability: Accounting for Strategic Disclosure. *Corporate Social Responsibility and Environmental Management.* 30(2), 802–819.

27 UN Office of the High Commissioner for Human Rights. "Promoting sustainable and inclusive growth in business" October 13, 2023. Available at https://www. ohchr.org/en/stories/2023/10/promoting-sustainable-and-inclusive-growth-business (accessed May 6, 2024).

INTRODUCTION

targets for the SDGs and good governance as two thirds of the formula, with business as the third variable. "It is the private sector which is the main motor of the world economy and which accounts for two-thirds of the use of our natural resources. Businesses, including small and medium-sized enterprises, have to drive the research and technological advances which are critical to overcoming the challenges I have talked about." He praises the innovation and entrepreneurial spirit of corporations. And then he concludes, "So businesses, as we see today, are increasingly realizing that corporate social responsibility is essential for their bottom-line. It can help deliver benefits which range from improved efficiency and larger markets to increased staff morale and public trust."[28] CSR is good for the world and good for business. It is a true win-win pitch in which business can be more profitable while helping to solve the problems of climate change, inequality, and inclusion of the historically marginalized.

These believers in the ability of corporations to act as agents for the greater good share certain assumptions. Chief among them is the belief that the people who work in businesses are motivated by the desire to do good and that they want to be seen as virtuous. They also suggest that the current policy or cultural environment is somehow preventing all of these altruistically oriented individuals from using their power and privilege for the benefit of humanity. All that's needed is the right incentive structure and CEOs will adopt policies that are good for the earth and all people. In fact, they will accelerate positive impact because in addition to their good intentions, they will bring their business savvy. The skills they use to make huge profits will be redirected to make huge impacts on poverty, pollution, and other such problems. Believers are deeply optimistic about the intentions and impact of CSR.

Nihilists, on the other hand, are critics of capitalism and corporations in particular. They see them as malign forces that cause most of the world's problems and see it as inevitable that involving corporations in the social sector will lead to greater harm. They anticipate that corporate representatives intend to gain positive publicity while continuing to exploit the marginalized and that corporate engagement will only benefit the corporation itself. There is a new and growing literature based on psychological experiments that show that the wealthy lack empathy, which leads them to misunderstand the social world and

---

28 Annan, Kofi. 2013. "Building healthy and sustainable societies through leadership, partnership and social responsibility" Kofi Annan Foundation. Copenhagen, DK. October 2013.

12   CORPORATE SOCIAL RESPONSIBILITY AND CIVIL SOCIETY

its needs.[29] I return to this rentier approach to understanding the decision-making by corporate and business owners in the concluding chapter.

Looking at the main arguments made by Nihilists, first they warn that CSR is a way to obscure the harm that businesses cause—all the negative externalities of pollution, unequal access to resources, overconsumption and so on are hidden behind "greenwashing" or "pinkwashing."[30] A second concern is that the provision of services by private actors—both corporate and civil society—can be a way for the state to abdicate its role and responsibility to its citizens. This is seen as part of a larger neoliberal assault on the state. Related, is the concern that philanthropic or corporate interventions in society are not democratic. That is, unlike elected governments, private reformers do not operate under any accountability mechanism. And finally, some point out that the technocratic approach to solving social problems that is the hallmark of corporate philanthropy reduces the space for democratic contestation over development decisions. That is, the politics of development is submerged under a torrent of impact assessment metrics such that there is no space to question the goals of economic development. Is faster growth truly what we need or want? Some exemplary Nihilistic arguments follow below.

Whitewash Corporate Harms

David Rieff, for example, argues that the worldview that sees private–public partnerships as the key to solving problems like the one of global hunger is bound to fail as it has become an article of faith and leaves no room for any alternatives. "Whatever the current developmentalist orthodoxy may be, the fundamental problems of the world have always been moral, not technological." Speaking of corporate foundations, he says "[…] their lack of accountability trumps those good intentions."[31] This is a condemnation of CSR based on a lack of faith in corporations to act in the public interest. Paying

---

29 Côté, S, J. House, and R. Willer. "High Economic Inequality Leads Higher-income Individuals to Be Less Generous." *Proc Natl Acad Sci U S A.* 2015 Dec 29; 112(52), 15838–15843; Suss, J. 2023. "Higher Income Individuals are More Generous When Local Economic Inequality is High." *PLoS One.* Jun 14; 18(6); Schmukle, S. C., M. Korndörfer, B. Egloff. "No Evidence that Economic Inequality Moderates the Effect of Income on Generosity." *Proc Natl Acad Sci U S A.* 2019 May 14; 116(20), 9790–9795.

30 NDRC. 2023. "What is Greenwashing?" Available at https://www.nrdc.org/stories/what-greenwashing and Puar, Jasbir. 2013. "Rethinking Homonationalism." *International Journal of Middle East Studies.* 45(2), 336–339.

31 Rieff, David. 2015. *The Reproach of Hunger: Food, Justice, and Money in the Twenty-first Century.* New York, NY: Simon & Schuster.

INTRODUCTION   13

taxes, rather than shielding their corporate income from taxes and offering philanthropy, would do more to actually end a problem like world hunger. In an early study of CSR in India, the authors acknowledged that, "Corporate self-regulation can also be viewed as an attempt to lessen the pressures from regulations and social responsibility."[32] That is, CSR can be a means to avoid greater scrutiny by the state and civil society. For instance CSR investment by extractive industries such as coal and mining can be characterized as an attempt to pacify and co opt local resistance to their operations.[33]

Replace Government

Kamat argues that neoliberal forces are pluralizing the public and depoliticizing the private spheres. CSOs (understood broadly to include industry lobbying associations and CSR bodies) pluralize our understanding of the public good/sphere to the point that we can't distinguish between actual private interests and the public good. The positioning of NGOs as a means to "empower" individuals to pull themselves out of poverty hides the structural forces that create poverty and depoliticize the private sphere. She writes that, "The neoliberal notion of empowerment implies a focus on individual capacities and needs of the poor, and consequently minimizing the social and political causes of poverty. The individual is posited as both the problem and solution to poverty rather than as an issue of the state's redistribution policies or global trade policies."[34] The growth in the visibility and power of both CSR representatives and CSOs work together in this formulation to undermine democratic accountability. The blurring of boundaries between private and public is especially harmful in tackling a problem like poverty. A similar concern is raised by Ritu Birla, who argues that the discourse of corporate philanthropy displaces metaphors of kinship and citizenship in favor of a patron-client relationship between the corporation and the people. Philanthropy becomes a technology of (neoliberal) governance through which "the rights of citizens are mediated by the responsibilities of corporations" who act as trustees of the nation's wealth. Objects of philanthropy are neither imagined through the intimacy of kinship and hierarchical mutuality of caste

---

32 Sood, Atul and Bimal Arora. 2006. "The political economy of CSR in India" UNRISD Publications: Issue 18.
33 Sunila S. Kale. 2020. "From Company Town to Company Village: CSR and the Management of Rural Aspirations in Eastern India's Extractive Economies." *The Journal of Peasant Studies*, 47(6), 1211–1232.
34 Kamat, Sangeeta. 2004. "The Privatization of Public Interest: Theorizing NGO Discourse in a Neoliberal Era." *Review of International Political Economy*. 11(1), 155–176.

14   CORPORATE SOCIAL RESPONSIBILITY AND CIVIL SOCIETY

nor the political boundaries of the nation, but as members of "communities that are understood as the environment of business."[35] That is, the existence of CSR enables corporations to forge new relationships of patronage to clients that displace the possibility of a relationship of corporate accountability to stakeholders or fellow-citizens.

Depoliticize Development Policy

Another concern with the win–win or technocratic approach to sustainable and inclusive development sponsored by a corporation is that it obscures the power dynamics that are part of any development program or paradigm. Instead of systems thinking, "the current paradigm depends on an engineering model in which a problem is defined, the best minds apply themselves to it, after honest and open debate a solution is arrived at, it is tried, and its success or failure is then quantified and measured."[36] This type of depoliticization has been identified in a broad range of development interventions.[37] Many bilateral donors and CSOs have learnt from this critique and adopted a different approach to development that places community participation at its center. However, with the CSR law, corporations are still at the beginning of learning why a technocratic approach is harmful.

Bornstein and Sharma suggest that, CSOs in India use a "technomoral politics" to make their claims on the state. "In mixing the languages of law and policy with moral pronouncements, state and non-state actors posture themselves as defenders of rights and keepers of the public interest as they push their agendas and stake out distinctive positions. 'Technomoral politics' refers to how various social actors translate moral projects into technical, implementable terms as laws or policies, as well as justify technocratic acts such as development and legislation regarding administrative reform- as moral imperatives." They found that, "Although corporate involvement represented potential alternate funding streams in the face of restricted foreign donations, NGO delegates were ambivalent." Because of different value systems, the CSO workers described selfless NGOs versus businesses driven by self-interest as incompatible partners. The anthropologists warn that, "In the process, CSR can redefine development in terms of capitalist aims and interests, extending the reach of the market, creating paternalistic

---

35 Birla, Ritu. 2018. C=f(P): The Trust, 'general public utility', and Charity as a Function of Profit in India. *Modern Asian Studies*, 52(1), 132–162.

36 Rieff, David. 2015. *The Reproach of Hunger: Food, Justice, and Money in the Twenty-first Century*. New York, NY: Simon & Schuster.

37 Ferguson, J. 1994. *The Anti-Politics Machine*. Stanford, CA: Stanford University Press.

INTRODUCTION   15

dependencies between corporations and CSR beneficiaries, and bestowing moral legitimacy on corporate and state actors." The CSR initiatives written into the Companies Act are an arena of technomoral politics where CSOs, corporations, and state institutions negotiate moral legitimacy.[38]

Historians of philanthropy observe that charity has always been political, it was never outside of politics. When new business elites engage in philanthropy, "[...] the moral discourse of benevolence not only engenders interventions that complement or replace altogether state welfare [...] but legitimizes and naturalizes class inequalities, and the privileges of elites whose philanthropic endeavors ostensibly trigger the trickle-down of wealth on society as a whole."[39] They describe the ways in which philanthropy has been a means to legitimize wealth accumulation for colonizing and native elites. These practices of extending aid built upon religious doctrine and allowed emerging elites to establish their trustworthiness, and build their political reputations. "The new philanthrocapitalism—which encompasses CSR- promises an alternative to state-led development, in which the social and environmental costs of rapid industrialization may well be ameliorated by business itself. CSR is often presented as a radical break from colonial forms of industrial philanthropy and post-colonial paternalism but, like its predecessors, it continues to be a means to negotiate relations with state and market, and to objectify pious dispositions."[40] The more things change, the more they stay the same.

The Middle Way[41]

In his quest for the deepest human knowledge, the Buddha is said to have discovered a "middle way" between the extremes of eternalism and nihilism. When faced with true believers on both sides he carefully considered the merits and demerits of their respective positions, fully adopting them to interrogate them and to test their mettle. He spent years as a prince in a palace, a true believer in the pleasures of the world as a path to happiness

---

38 Bornstein, Erica and Aradhana Sharma. 2016 "The Righteous and the Rightful: The Technomoral Politics of NGOs, Social Movements, and the State in India." *American Ethnologist.* 43, 76–90.

39 Osella, Filippo. 2018. "Charity and Philanthropy in South Asia: An Introduction." *Modern Asian Studies.* 52(1), 4–34.

40 Osella, Filippo. 2018. "Charity and Philanthropy in South Asia: An Introduction." *Modern Asian Studies.* 52(1), 4–34.

41 Gethin, Rupert. 1998. *The Foundations of Buddhsim.* Oxford: Oxford University Press. pp. 165.

16   CORPORATE SOCIAL RESPONSIBILITY AND CIVIL SOCIETY

and then subsequently, as an ascetic renunciate, seeking truth by completely rejecting his life of luxury. In the end, by forging a path between these two extremes he found what Buddhists now refer to as enlightenment, or a deep understanding of the ways things truly are. His middle path drew on aspects of both of those earlier paths, his experiences in the palace informing his deep commitment to compassion and his renunciation producing the necessary wisdom to see how things truly are and to act effectively in the world. I came to this project inspired by this example, hoping to find a middle path, a complex story in which there are identifiable conditions under which corporate–civil society collaborations can work toward sustainable and inclusive development. Having studied civil society for two decades, I am aware of its diversity, its limitations, and how it operates within shifting constraints imposed by resource needs and political structures.[42] Having written previously about how foreign aid partnerships and transnational networks can both enable and curtail civil society action, I thought that both the Believer and Nihilist position was too simplistic. Surely, sometimes corporations can be good partners?

I truly wanted to identify the conditions under which corporate–civil society collaborations could succeed. Believers seemed a bit too sanguine about the good intentions of corporations and their ability to apply their business lens to solving sticky social problems. Meanwhile, the Nihilists seemed to be so pessimistic and hopeless that anything good could come from corporate attention to social problems that I thought they must be overlooking something. And I think they were. I think the Believers are correct that the individuals who work at corporations generally want to make a positive impact on the world. They want it to be true that they can do good and do well at the same time. However, the Nihilists are also right that corporations entering the development space are not actually helping solve these challenges. Despite their good intentions, their impact is negative.

Why? This book answers this question by looking at the historical development of civil society and corporations, the policy environment in India, and through many case studies and stories from the actors involved in CSR and civil society collaborations. Most succinctly, these partnerships fail because the core design of these two different types of organizations are incompatible. It's like trying to shove a square peg into a round hole. The different purposes of these organizations cannot be denied. The differences in how corporations

---

42 See for example Deo, Nandini and Duncan McDuie Ra. 2011. *The Politics of Collective Advocacy in India*. New York: Lynn Reinner; Deo, Nandini. 2016. *Mobilizing Religion and Gender in India*. London: Routledge.

INTRODUCTION

and civil society organizations relate to the people they serve is one important distinction. The impersonality of a corporation as a legal and economic actor contrasts with the emotional and moral relations a CSO builds with its community partners. Efficiency is a virtue in the business world but can be a source of failure for a civil society organization. And the time horizons of quarterly, or even annual, impact assessments that corporate boards embrace are anathema to most social work organizations. Each of these characteristics will be explored in detail in the coming chapters.

Outline of the Book

This introductory chapter inaugurates the reader to the politics of CSR and its engagement with civil society organizations in India. I locate the interdisciplinary scholarship that this book engages; the literature on development, corporations and philanthropy, and on the changing nature of civil society organizations. I offer two contrasting perspectives on CSR; the Believers and the Nihilists and explain why I hoped to find a middle path between them. I conclude by offering a glimpse of my conclusion and discussing the significance of my findings.

Chapter 1 explores the historical development of corporations and nonprofit organizations. I identify the strengths and weaknesses of each of these organizational forms and highlight key differences. This leads to a discussion of how we may expect these distinct types of actors to mutually benefit from collaboration. Often some divergence in strengths is needed for a partnership to truly add value. Is that the case in corporate and civil society partnerships? I conclude with a consideration of how each of these organization types embodies its own set of (largely incompatible) values.

Chapter 2 delves into the legal development of mandatory CSR in India. I begin with the puzzle of how this legislation was conceived and passed in the absence of any voluble constituency demanding it. I argue that the passage of Article 135 is an instance of the state attempting to regulate business rather than an abdication of its own role in society as some critics contend. In this chapter, I describe the policies themselves in some detail.

In Chapter 3, the book examines the universal framework of inclusive and sustainable development as an attempt to articulate a vision of our life on Earth beyond mass consumerism. Much of the chapter is taken up by describing the various dimensions of inequality and exclusion that shape the patterns of privilege and deprivation in India. I show how these dimensions are interconnected in ways that make solving social problems using a technocratic and narrow approach hopelessly doomed. Instead, deep and transformative engagements are needed to move beyond the discrimination and deprivation

18   CORPORATE SOCIAL RESPONSIBILITY AND CIVIL SOCIETY

that exists today. Power is a critical aspect of development and must be part of any intervention's theory of change.

Chapter 4 returns to the Believer's vision for what mandatory CSR could accomplish. This vision is contrasted with the reality of what CSR and civil society collaborations actually do in a series of case studies. The short-term horizons, the focus on output rather than outcome, and the relentless marketing of even minor programs are common. This runs counter to the deep and transformative changes that Chapter 3 showed are needed to achieve inclusive and sustainable development.

Chapter 5 centers the perspectives of civil society leaders and workers as they describe the challenges they face in collaborating with corporations. By using the framework of public and hidden transcripts, I show that these collaborations are more like patron–client relations than partnerships of equals. The financial dependence of CSOs on corporations makes them into supplicants rather than partners. The exceptions are the few cases when a CSR representative has crossed over from the social sector themselves. Many civil society workers have also moved into the consulting arena, helping corporations and CSOs find matches and navigate their collaborations. This is a kind of "brain drain" from the civil society sector into the corporate sector.

And finally in the "Conclusion," I describe the corporatization of civil society as the outcome of the past decade of mandatory CSR. The amount of money at play has distorted the traditional relationships between corporations and civil society. A discussion of alternative pathways to inclusive and sustainable development leads to a consideration of the future after democratic decline and corporate dominance.

Significance

This book does not provide the insights I had hoped to discover about the conditions under which corporations and civil society organizations can collaborate to advance sustainable and inclusive development. In that sense, if the reader is looking for a tidy answer that identifies one side as good and the other side as bad, it may be a real disappointment. So, why should you bother to read it? It is worth reading to understand why CSR is not the means to solving our pressing challenges. The fact that I avoid the strong assumptions of the Believers and the Nihilists makes me a more credible guide to exploring the impact of CSR on civil society. I did not have a particular perspective for which I sought confirming evidence, rejecting experiences that failed to conform to my ideology. Instead, my conclusions are based on the messy reality I encountered over a decade of observing and analyzing this subject.

My finding that CSR is not a means to sustainable and inclusive development suggests that civil society organizations that are committed to this work need to think beyond how to make themselves attractive to corporate donors. It means that we should consider repealing Article 135 in favor of a return to voluntary CSR for those select companies who truly want to do it to improve employee morale, or for marketing purposes, or for whatever whimsy moves their executive board. Instead, we should advocate for more robust taxation of corporate profits, greater internalization of externalities into product pricing, and a reduction in the regulation of the civil society sector. We need civil society to speak truth to power. CSR money makes it much harder for them to do so. And the public celebration of corporate beneficence makes it harder for civil society to question the growth model offered by mainstream economists.

Chapter 1
CORPORATIONS AND CIVIL SOCIETY ORGANIZATIONS

Painting commissioned for ceiling of EIC offices from British Library, CC0, via Wikimedia Commons

In 1599, a motley group of investors, interested in exploring and engaging in trade beyond the East Indies, raised funds and petitioned the Queen of England to grant them a license to form the East India Company. They were inspired by the success of the Dutch East India Company, which was making fortunes from the sale of spices collected in Indonesia and Malaysia and sold in European markets at a 400% profit. In 1600, their petition was granted. In the first few decades, the Company largely engaged in trade and negotiated access to Indian ports as supplicants to Mughal rulers. The following decades

22   CORPORATE SOCIAL RESPONSIBILITY AND CIVIL SOCIETY

saw a slow and steady rise of influence and by 1693, the Company was wealthy and powerful enough to be caught in a widespread bribery investigation in which they were paying British MPs regular sums to maintain their monopoly over trade in India. In the early eighteenth century, their fortunes in India were threatened by internal wars between Emperor Aurangzeb and the Maratha King Shivaji. These wars led to instability and rising crime in Central and Western India and, as a consequence, the Company switched its primary trade focus to Eastern India watching as the Persian Emperor Nader Shah weakened the Mughals in 1732.[1] The battles between Nader Shah and the Mughal armies significantly contributed to the conditions necessary for European colonial intervention. The success of Robert Clive as military commander in the 1757 Battle of Plassey is the commonly agreed upon start to British colonialism in India—a battle sparked by the Company's refusal to pay taxes. This victory gave the Company the power to levy taxes on local trade and shifted the mission of the corporation from one of monopolistic trade to that of a rapacious empire.[2] Another century later, as its trade was threatened by competitors, a rebellion by Indian soldiers led the Company to relinquish formal control over India to the British crown, which augmented the Company's troops to quell the "mutiny."[3] By this time, the Company's efforts toward resource extraction and profit-making had created deep and lasting shifts across the subcontinent, from its engagement in the Opium Wars, in which it illegally peddled opium from India to China to access Chinese tea for trade,[4] to the unsustainable tax burdens it placed on Indian farmers, which forced many to become indentured laborers, sent all over the British empire from Fiji to Guyana to South Africa to work in plantations that no longer could operate with African slave labor alone.[5]

---

1 Dalrymple, William. 2019. *The Anarchy: The Relentless Rise of the East India Company.* London, UK: Bloomsbury.

2 Erikson, Emily. 2014. *Between Monopoly and Free Trade: The English East India Company, 1600–1757.* Princeton, NJ: Princeton University Press; Stern, P. 2011. *The Company-State: Corporate Sovereignty and the Early Modern Foundations of the British Empire in India.* Oxford, UK: Oxford University Press.

3 Erikson, Emily. 2014. *Between Monopoly and Free Trade: The English East India Company, 1600–1757.* Princeton, NJ: Princeton University Press.

4 Hevia, J. L. 2003. "Opium, Empire, and Modern History" [*Review of Modern China and Opium: A Reader; Opium Regimes: China, Britain, and Japan, 1839–1952; Britain's China Policy and the Opium Crisis: Balancing Drugs, Violence and National Honour, 1833–1840; Opium, Empire, and the Global Political Economy: A Study of the Asian Opium Trade 1750–1950,* by A. Baumler, T. Brook, B. T. Wakabayashi, G. Melancon, & C. A. Trocki]. *China Review International,* 10(2), 307–326.

5 Sen, S. 2016. "Indentured Labour from India in the Age of Empire." *Social Scientist,* 44(1/2), 35–74.

CORPORATIONS AND CIVIL SOCIETY ORGANIZATIONS 23

After the British crown took over India, these practices continued, and new horrors were added. This is the era of Indian deindustrialization in which raw cotton was exported to feed mills in Liverpool and Manchester while Indian weavers were collaterally put out of business.[6]

Through taxes, monopolies, trade regulations, and the threat of violence, the Indian economy was systematically destroyed so that the British economy could be turbocharged. The effects of this chapter of globalization were profound, and they continue into the present. A strong Indian aversion to corporate power and a recognition of the potential violence associated with "free trade" are some of the marks left by this legacy. How this legacy was overcome in the twentieth century to turn the Indian state and population from being wary of big business to embracing large corporations is a vital question.

This history of the East India Company is also important for making sense of the origins of the corporation in world history.[7] While prior to the rise of the English and Dutch East India Companies, there were a variety of methods for investors to pool assets and risks as they engaged in commerce, the creation of these entities marks a new chapter in the management of long-distance production. Unlike the *commendas* used by Mediterranean traders, or Arab *qirada*, these entities had the characteristic of being impersonal. That is, they did not depend on the personal charisma or kinship networks of the traders, sailors, and investors to facilitate cooperation. In this sense, these companies are the wellspring of today's corporations.

In this book, I use the term corporations loosely to refer to any of the variety of profit-oriented production enterprises that are legally recognized as businesses. When speaking specifically about public sector enterprises or benefit corporations as distinct varieties of corporations, I will use those terms. In a similar vein, I use the term "civil society organization" (CSO) broadly to refer to nonprofit organizations that include foundations, trusts, charities, and so on. CSOs or NGOs are also not all entirely nongovernmental as some are sponsored by the state, or subcontract various duties from it, or accept funding from it. What follows is an attempt to define what corporations and CSOs are in historical terms, in functional terms, and in relation to one another in India.

---

6 Parthasarathi, Prasannan. 2011. *Why Europe Grew Rich and Asia Did Not: Global Economic Divergence, 1600–1850.* Cambridge: Cambridge University Press.

7 Robins, N. 2012. *The Corporation that Changed the World : How the East India Company Shaped the Modern Multinational.* London: Pluto Press.

24   CORPORATE SOCIAL RESPONSIBILITY AND CIVIL SOCIETY

Corporations can be thought of as possessing seven distinctive traits:

1. Separate legal personality
2. Collective decision making
3. Financed through joint-stock equity
4. Locked in investment
5. Transferability of shares in the corporation
6. Protection from state expropriation
7. Asset partitioning to protect investors' private assets

The coalescence of these traits led to an "organizational revolution," which enabled commerce on a new scale, according to legal historian Ron Harris.[8] By treating assets as protected and separate, investors can take much bigger risks while limited liability separates the corporation from other varieties of partnership. Perhaps the impersonality of the corporation is both the source of its great success in mobilizing capital *and* also what enables it to disregard the effects of its business practices on human beings.

There is a long-standing debate, central to the arguments explored in this book, over who the corporation serves—shareholders, employees, consumers, or society itself?[9] To this end, Milton Freidman[10] famously declared that "there is one and only one social responsibility of business—to use its resources and engage in activities designed to increase its profits so long as it stays within the rules of the game, which is to say, engages in open and free competition without deception [or] fraud." He argued further that, "the doctrine of 'social responsibility' involves the acceptance of the socialist view that political mechanisms, not market mechanisms, are the appropriate way to determine the allocation of scarce resources to alternative uses." And he insists that this argument applies especially to large corporations whose executives must only seek profit while the owners of small businesses themselves may have a broader understanding of what constitutes the goals and means of that enterprise.[11] Already in 1970, he wrote this essay as a counter to businessmen who argued that firms do have a social responsibility beyond profit maximization.

---

8 Harris, Ron. 2020. *Going the Distance: Eurasian Trade and the Rise of the Business Corporation, 1400–1700*. The Princeton Economic History of the Western World Series. Princeton, NJ: Princeton University Press. p. 252.

9 Gindis, David. 2020. "Conceptualizing the Business Corporation: Insights from History." *Journal of Institutional Economics*. 16(5), 569–577.

10 Among others, Naomi Klein provides a searing indictment of Milton Friedman and his ideas in her 2007 book *Shock Doctrine*. London, UK: Picador.

11 Friedman, Milton. 1970. "A Friedman Doctrine—The Social Responsibility of Business Is to Increase Its Profits." *The New York Times*. September 13, 1970.

CORPORATIONS AND CIVIL SOCIETY ORGANIZATIONS   25

Since then, in the United States, the premise advanced in his argument has only grown in acceptance and, thanks to the Citizens United ruling in particular, the idea that corporations are in fact endowed with legal personhood has made great strides.[12] In India, corporate law is partially converging with regulations found in the Anglo-American world.[13] The Companies Act governs corporations and is implemented by the Ministry for Corporate Affairs and the Ministry of Finance, which regulates the 365 public sector enterprises that are wholly or partially owned by the Indian state.[14] The 2013 revisions to the Companies Act are discussed in some detail in Chapter 2 For now, we look at the origins and legal status of CSOs.

Civil society organizations and social movements have existed alongside the modern state since its inception, and they have engaged in politics across national boundaries for just as long.[15] Broadly, these are voluntary groups that are not engaged in electoral politics themselves, that do not seek to make profits, and that can be based on shared identity or commitments. They include unions, neighborhood associations, amateur sports leagues, caste associations, advocacy groups, charitable organizations, and so on.[16] During the 1990s, these organizations became more and more prominent in everyday life and also drew increasing scholarly attention. Their role in bringing about the demise of authoritarian rule in Eastern Europe and Latin America, their inclusion in development planning by multilateral institutions, and the professionalization of social movement associations of feminists, environmentalists, and others, in large part drove this visibility. Studies of civic engagement and its effects on democracy[17] and ethnic conflict[18] showed

---

12 https://www.fec.gov/resources/legal-resources/litigation/cu_sc08_opinion.pdf.

13 Afsharipour, Afra. 2009. "Corporate Governance Convergence: Lessons from the Indian Experience" *Northwest Journal of Law and Business*. 29(2), 335–402; Kar, P. 2016. "Cogitations on Corporate Governance: When It Began, How It Began, and Where Is It Now." In *Corporate Governance in India: Change and Continuity*. Oxford, UK: Oxford University Press.

14 Government of India. "Public Enterprises Survey 2019–2020" Ministry of Finance, New Delhi. Available at https://dpe.gov.in/sites/default/files/PE_Survery_Vol_II_English_2019_20_0.pdf (accessed May 23, 2022).

15 Keck, M. and Sikkink, K. 1998. *Activists Beyond Borders*. Ithaca, NY: Cornell University Press; Tilly, C. and Tarrow, S. 2015. *Contentious Politics*. 2nd edition. Oxford, UK: Oxford University Press.

16 Skocpol, T. 2013. *Diminished Democracy: From Membership to Management in American Civic Life*. Norman, OK: University of Oklahoma Press.

17 Putnam, R. 2000. *Bowling Alone*. New York, NY: Simon & Schuster.

18 Varshney, A. 2002. *Ethnic Conflict and Civic Life*. New Haven, CT: Yale University Press.

26   CORPORATE SOCIAL RESPONSIBILITY AND CIVIL SOCIETY

that the presence or absence of these voluntary associations had significant impacts on politics. Much of this literature builds on Tocqueville's analysis of American democracy and further extends it to other times and places.[19] What are the core features of CSOs and what is their status in Indian law?

To define CSOs, we can look to these three features as significant:

1. Independent of the state
2. Nonprofit
3. Voluntary

Independence from the state is not absolute as there are a variety of CSO–state partnership models, but CSOs are not state agencies in a legal sense. They are nonprofit organizations, which means they do not operate on a profit-maximizing basis. They often do, however, need to develop fundraising strategies that can mimic market practices. Finally, they are voluntary in that membership relies on a desire for engagement, although many have paid employees. While there was some debate in the early 2000s over whether only voluntary associations "count" and those based on ascriptive identities don't (e.g., caste or ethnic associations), this has largely been resolved by social scientists to include both.[20]

In terms of their legal status, CSOs in India are registered as trusts, societies, or a special class of company. Trusts are required to serve the public, and their objectives are permanent as long as they are operating and controlling any assets, while societies are more flexible in terms of revising their objectives. Both trusts and societies are governed by state law while a Section 8 Company, the third category, is supposed to serve the public interest as a nonprofit and is governed by the Ministry of Corporate Affairs at the central government. This last category makes fundraising, particularly from foreign donors, less cumbersome. All three types of organization are covered by the Foreign Contributions Regulation Act (FCRA) regulations (discussed in detail in Chapter 2).

The number of registered CSOs skyrocketed over the first decade of the twenty-first century. In 2001, estimates for the number of CSOs in India were around 30,000,[21] and by 2009, the Asian Development Bank

---

19 Tocqueville, Alexis de, 1805–1859. (1838). *Democracy in America*. New York: G. Dearborn & Co.
20 Varshney, A. 2002. *Ethnic Conflict and Civic Life*. New Haven, CT: Yale University Press.
21 Baviskar, B. S. 2001. "CSOs and Civil Society in India." *Sociological Bulletin*, 50(1), 3–15.

CORPORATIONS AND CIVIL SOCIETY ORGANIZATIONS   27

estimated their number to be 1.5 million.[22] This pace of acceleration only continued into 2010 with the Central Bureau of Investigation, estimating that there are about 3.1 million registered CSOs as of 2014.[23] These numbers could be deceptive though, as there is no mechanism to deregister a CSO in Indian law. It is understood that a significant percentage of these are actually defunct organizations, and most of these organizations are quite small with about two-thirds operating with a staff of just one or two persons. Many of the trends discussed in this book will be about the one-third of CSOs that are larger, that have the capacity to carry out multiyear projects, and that operate on the basis of some standardized procedures rather than the entirely ad hoc and episodic work that characterizes the one-person shops.

Social Roles

What roles do corporations and CSOs play in society? Answering this requires us to consider both the intentional activities they engage in, as well as the unintended or latent effects they have on society. Describing these roles allows us to consider the relative contributions of these organizations and the skills they bring to the table in creating the partnerships that are a focus of this book.

As briefly mentioned already, one of the key roles of the corporation is to maximize profits for shareholders. This work of generating wealth for investors is either the sole or the most important intentional function of a corporation.[24] In addition to this, a number of scholars and practitioners argue that corporations have broader social responsibilities. This view is often described using the language of the "triple bottom line," where in addition to profit (the first bottom line), capitalist firms prioritize people and environment as two additional "bottom lines," or the language of "corporate social responsibility."[25]

---

22 Samaj, P. 2009. "Civil Society Brief: India" Asian Development Bank. Available at https://www.adb.org/sites/default/files/publication/28966/csb-ind.pdf (accessed May 26, 2022).

23 Anand, U. 2015. "India has 31 lakh CSOs." *Indian Express.* August 1.

24 Mankiw, N. G. 2016. *Principles of Microeconomics.* 8th edition. Boston, MA: Cengage Learning Custom Publishing.

25 Padro, M. 2014. "Unpacking Corporate Purpose." *Aspen Institute Report.* Available at https://www.aspeninstitute.org/wp-content/uploads/files/content/docs/pubs/Unpacking%20Corporate%20Purpose%20May%202014.pdf (accessed May 29, 2022).

28   CORPORATE SOCIAL RESPONSIBILITY AND CIVIL SOCIETY

In a basic sense, in order to create profits, firms have to sell a product that people want to pay money for. That means they engage in innovation and production—thereby offering new products to discerning consumers. In addition to the conscious and intentional pursuit of profit through the supply of innovative and valued products, corporations also are thought to serve important roles in society that are essentially a byproduct of this pursuit. The "invisible hand of the market" is supposed to accomplish an efficient division of resources within society. While Adam Smith's phrase has come to stand in as a core tenet of free market ideology, there is some evidence that he used it ironically and was actually much more concerned about promoting social welfare than unfettered capitalism.[26] Nonetheless, in common understanding, the invisible hand of the market is supposed to produce accurate prices (for products and labor) as well as assign resources in the most productive ways. That is, in pursuit of the greatest possible profit for their shareholders, managers within a corporation are incentivized to discover how to please their customers and price their goods so as to maximize income. Many firms pursuing this goal allow investors to invest in the corporations that achieve these goals in the most efficient way. This selective investment process in the aggregate leads investment and production resources to the areas of the economy, which are producing the goods or services most valued by customers.

Businesses are often credited with being major employers and wealth creators. Cheerleaders of global capitalism like Jagdish Bhagwati and Steven Pinker argue that businesses are benevolent forces because they generate wealth through the production of goods and services, they make people better off as consumers, and they encourage investment in the health and education of the population to make them better workers.[27] The roles of corporations as employers and wealth creators are central to their public political power.

Even someone like Pinker, however, acknowledges that corporations embedded within capitalism produce inequality. And while he argues that inequality is not a problem, other researchers convincingly show that inequality in itself is harmful to economic growth and human flourishing.[28]

---

26 Rothschild, E. 1994. "Adam Smith and the Invisible Hand." *The American Economic Review*, 84(2), 319–322.

27 Bhagwati, J. 2004. *Defense of Globalization*. Oxford, UK: Oxford University Press; Pinker, S. 2018. *Enlightenment Now*. New York, NY: Viking.

28 Ahmad, N., Marriott, A., Dabi, N., Lowthers, M., Lawson, M., and Mugehera, L. 2022. Inequality Kills. *Oxfam International*. Available at https://oxfamilibrary. openrepository.com/bitstream/handle/10546/621341/bp-inequality-kills-170122-en.pdf (accessed May 29 2022).

CORPORATIONS AND CIVIL SOCIETY ORGANIZATIONS 29

Inequality is an inevitable byproduct of an economic system, which relies on "creative destruction," the constant churn that leads to the replacement of one production process by another.[29] It is creative because it produces new products and processes but destructive because it makes existing products and processes obsolete. Those things, processes, and skills that are made obsolete result in companies going under, shops closing, and skilled workers becoming redundant. There are winners and losers. Therefore, inequality is a necessary aspect of the capitalist mode of production. In India, growth and inequality have a strong correlation.[30]

Besides inequality as a natural effect of, and internal to, normal business practice, there are all of the externalities that business produces. Externalities are all the side effects of a business process that are not factored into the price of the product being sold and that impact bystanders without their consent. Chapter 3 discusses externalities in detail. For now, we can simply flag the destruction of ecosystems through industrial pollution, deforestation, heavy water use, emissions, and the negative health effects of all of these as significant externalities produced by corporations.

Finally, and perhaps more controversially, there is the culture of materialism and consumption that is an externalized effect of corporate activity. The huge sums spent on advertising and marketing attest to the need to constantly create markets for products. That is, often businesses produce goods or services that no one knows they need or want. The maker of the product then has to create an artificial demand for that product.[31] To market to consumers directly, corporations create a fiction that the consumer is not whole without that product and the self-hatred, doubt, and alienation that the consumer economy relies on is a major externality of corporate activity that is rarely included in analyses of what corporations add to society.[32] The reduction of citizens to consumers is then a danger to other visions of human sociality represented by democracy, religion, feminism, and other varieties of solidarity.

---

29 Schumpeter, J. A. 2008. *Capitalism, Socialism and Democracy*. New York, NY: Harper Perennial (1950).

30 Dang, H. A. H. and Lanjouw, P. 2018. "Inequality in India on the Rise." *WIDER Policy Brief* 2018/6. Helsinki: UNU-WIDER. Available at https://www.wider.unu.edu/publication/inequality-india-rise.

31 Glaser, R., Sandor, R., Shiller, R., and Podolny, J. 2007. "What does it take to create a market?" *Yale Insights*. Available at https://insights.som.yale.edu/insights/what-does-it-take-to-create-market (accessed May 30, 2022).

32 Stuppy, A., Mead, N., and Van Osselaer, S., 2020. "I Am, Therefore I Buy: Low Self-Esteem and the Pursuit of Self-Verifying Consumption." *Journal of Consumer Research*. 46(5), 956–973.

30   CORPORATE SOCIAL RESPONSIBILITY AND CIVIL SOCIETY

Now we turn to the social roles of CSOs. As mentioned above, the term CSO refers to a wide range of organizations that also have a variety of relationships with governments. In fact, it can be argued that the CSO is defined in terms of a series of negatives—it is not a government, it is not profit-seeking, and so on. However, we can also think of it in a more affirmative sense, as Bernal and Grewal have argued, "the NGO form produces and converts what is outside the state into a legible form within a governmentality that parallels official state power."[33] That is, CSOs are a type of mini-bureaucracy that mimics the state but deals with the issues and people that the state doesn't want to or isn't capable of governing. CSOs, as disciplinary organizations that create and operate within discourses of power, produce "empowered women," "environmentally sustainable tribes," and so on. These are subjects that can then be fit into broader neoliberal governmentalities. In this way of thinking about CSOs, we see that they are not of the state but they are not necessarily in opposition to the state either.

Within liberal democratic frameworks, CSOs are theorized as offering an alternative to the state and the market by acting as "watchdogs."[34] They are expected to independently monitor the powerful and offer constructive criticism, which helps keep these power centers honest and accountable to the people in between elections. This is the democracy-promoting aspect of CSOs that was most celebrated in the 1990s. Their ability to mobilize people to exercise moral authority over authoritarian or semi-democratic states helped usher in the post-Communist transitions in Eastern Europe and Latin America.[35] CSOs were identified as the key to democracy in the coming century.

Within a Habermasian framework, CSOs are a space in which interests are discovered and aggregated by ordinary people. That is, rather than thinking of CSOs as being in opposition to the state, this tradition imagines civil society as a space in which we discover our preferences and form our identities. This process leads to the bubbling up of the goals of society and politics. CSOs are critical to a healthy society because they are the pathway for the unrepresented to achieve inclusion.[36]

---

33 Bernal, V. and Grewal, I. (eds). 2014. *Theorizing CSOs*. Durham, NC: Duke University Press. p. 8.

34 Edwards, M. 1996. *Beyond the Magic Bullet: CSO Performance and Accountability*. New York, NY: Lynn Reinner.

35 Cohen, J. and Arato, A. 1992. *Civil Society and Political Theory*. Boston, MA: MIT Press.

36 Edwards, M. 1996. *Beyond the Magic Bullet: CSO Performance and Accountability*. New York, NY: Lynn Reinner.

CORPORATIONS AND CIVIL SOCIETY ORGANIZATIONS   31

The goodwill and legitimacy granted to CSOs also rely on their self-representation as more efficient and nimbler than states in service provision.[37] They offer themselves as better able to reach those who are outside the ambit of the public state—women, children, historically marginalized groups, the disabled, and so on. CSOs claim that they can reach these constituencies and articulate their needs. Once those needs are identified, they also should be more efficient at servicing those needs. Advocacy and service provision are often combined, and the lines between welfare and political work are blurry. Their claims to efficiency of course also imply that states are not efficient and that efficiency is a high priority. This approach ignores that state provision of public goods is meant to be fully inclusive, and that the pursuit of inclusivity is part of what makes states "inefficient." Many programs that work well on a small scale grow inefficient or bureaucratic when deployed at mass scale.

A difficulty in our conception of CSOs is that they are not always civil or efficient at representing the marginalized. CSOs can build solidarity and mobilize even on the basis of out-group exclusion and violence as seen in the examples of the Nazi movement in 1930s Germany[38] or Hindutva groups in contemporary India.[39] These civic associations are the opposite of the inclusive, equity-oriented organizations that we expect CSOs to be.

Further, CSOs are often constrained by their donors in ways that also distort their ability to represent the marginalized groups for whom they work.[40] That is, the pursuit of grant funding forces CSOs to adopt the framing and language of donor agencies, which can lead them away from the concerns of their grassroots members or beneficiaries. This can mean that instead of a focus on women's inheritance rights to land, a group emphasizes sexual rights in order to secure funding.[41] Or it may lead a group to adopt a focus on ending child marriage rather than broader security concerns caused by a foreign occupation or civil conflict.[42] Either way, the work that is being done is imperfectly representative of the preferences of the group the CSO claims

---

37 Bernal, V. and Grewal, I. (eds). 2014. *Theorizing CSOs*. Durham, NC: Duke University Press. p. 8.

38 Berman, S. 1997. Civil Society and the Collapse of the Weimar Republic. *World Politics*, 49(3), 401–429.

39 Deo, N. 2018. *Mobilizing Religion and Gender in India*. London, UK: Routledge.

40 Deo, N. and McDuie Ra, D. 2011. *The Politics of Collective Advocacy in India*. Boulder, CO: Lynne Reinner.

41 Basu, A. 2000. "Globalization of the Local/Localization of the Global: Mapping Transnational Women's Movements." *Meridians*. 1(1), 68–84.

42 Kandiyoti, D. 2007. "Between the Hammer and the Anvil: Post-Conflict Reconstruction, Islam and Women's Rights." *Third World Quarterly*, 28(3), 503–517.

32   CORPORATE SOCIAL RESPONSIBILITY AND CIVIL SOCIETY

to speak for or work for and instead it is forced to adopt the priorities or methods of its funding agencies.

The most troubling concern raised about the rise to prominence of CSOs is the hidden curriculum their appearance represents. As CSOs started being embraced by development agencies, James Ferguson suggested they are "anti-politics machines."[43] That is, they take politically contentious decisions about how to use and distribute resources within a community and convert them into technocratic and bureaucratic processes. Thus, the process by which winners and losers are created becomes hidden. CSOs also can come to compete with the state as they control more and more resources. As their power and resources grow, they can make political parties and electoral rules seem irrelevant to people's lives. CSOs can end up undermining democracy rather than promoting it.[44]

The depoliticization of decision-making in development is a major concern. The biggest questions are ones about what is needed for a good life and how we organize our societies to achieve good lives. When these questions are treated as if we all already know the answers or that all we need to do is figure out the means because the ends are obvious, that leaves us foreclosing the option to reject a consumer-driven materialism. In this way, while CSOs hold out the promise of offering alternative and more humane visions for human societies, they can also serve to narrow the imagination of what is possible.

Historical Relationship between Corporations and CSOs

Corporations and CSOs share one feature—they are not part of the public state and they are not part of the private sphere of the family. Instead, they are intermediary institutions that connect individuals to others beyond the family for a variety of end goals. While corporate goals include the production of a profit, and CSOs are explicitly nonprofit, both do have to figure out how to raise enough funds to sustain their operations. The process by which corporations do this involves their creation and marketing of goods and services. For CSOs, it involves the creation and marketing of a vision and services.

Each type of organization offers differing visions for how humans can work together and the ends to which we can aspire. Where the corporation brings

---

43 Ferguson, J. 1994. *The Anti-Politics Machine.* Milwaukee, MN: University of Minnesota Press.

44 Banks, N., Hulme, D., and Edwards, M. 2015. "CSOs, states, and donors revisited: Still too close for comfort?" *World Development.* 66, 707–718.

CORPORATIONS AND CIVIL SOCIETY ORGANIZATIONS   33

people together through commercial relationships as employers, employees, consumers, and investors, the CSO speaks the language of stakeholders, donors, members, employers, employees, and beneficiaries. In the corporate world, the conception of individuals is that of *homo economicus*—a person who is autonomous and able to engage in voluntary exchanges based on their individually formed preferences.[45] People generally maximize their self-interest, and the goal of the organization is to be as efficient as possible at making a profit. The vision for society is of a wide variety of people and organizations pursuing their own interests, with continuous growth based on greater consumption and ease. Behavioral economics has become increasingly mainstream[46] in its critique of this model of how humans make decisions, but elements of this ideology persist, especially in normative ideas about how people and the world *should* behave. Pursuit of self-interest, endless growth, and profit maximizing are the signs of a healthy society in the corporate world.

The CSO world offers a different ideological frame, even if in practice, sometimes it is not so different from the corporate world. In the CSO vision of humans, they are deeply embedded within social relations with identities and obligations that stem from these relationships. These identities and social roles shape the preferences and interests of people in ways that are not commensurable or universal which means that each person can be pursuing their own definition of a good life in ways that are completely unrecognizable to another. The ideal society is one that supports these multiple life projects which may require massive social change to achieve, and how conflicts among projects are to be adjudicated is usually left unsaid. The pursuit of life plans, with economic and political rules arranged to enable them, is central to a healthy society in the CSO world.

These alternative visions are in tension with each other. In the corporate world, growth and self-interest are guiding principles. In the CSO world, meaning and relationships are their guiding principles. These are broad generalizations, and there are bound to be many exceptions, but I think, these distinctions capture the animating spirit of each of these spheres. The tensions in terms of how human beings are conceptualized lead to stark differences in what is considered valuable or even essential for a society. They also lead each of these sectors to regard each other as a threat.

---

45 Persky, J. 1995. "Retrospectives: The Ethology of *Homo Economicus*." *The Journal of Economic Perspectives*. 9(2), 221–231.

46 Fox, Justin. 2015. "From 'Economic Man' to Behavioral Economics" *Harvard Business Review*. May. Available at https://hbr.org/2015/05/from-economic-man-to-behavioral-economics (accessed June 6, 2022).

34   CORPORATE SOCIAL RESPONSIBILITY AND CIVIL SOCIETY

"Even though the NGO sector has emerged as a big force in the last few decades in India, somehow coming from the corporate sector they still want to come with their own cultural norms, norms of efficiency, value for money, numbers, all these things matter to them. Software, investing in people, processes, principles, those matter a lot [to CSOs]. So there is a kind of cultural clash which will take time to evolve [...]"[47] The director of this water and sanitation CSO describes the culture clash that prevents corporations and CSOs from partnering with each other.

Mistrust is a long-standing feature of corporate and CSO relations with each other in India, largely based on their distance from each other.[48] There is a wide literature that demonstrates the benefits of trust between organizations. Networks with high levels of trust have a number of benefits. "Where there is mutual trust, actors tend to interact and share information and knowledge more freely; information asymmetries, risk of opportunism and transaction cost are lower; and shared values, norms, and attitudes tend to develop."[49] In the absence of trust, organizations hoard information, engage in competitive rather than collaborative behavior, and can even find themselves working at cross-purposes. A key pathway to building trust is through repeated interactions as a result of proximity. That is, repeated encounters and cooperation over time can build trust.

Corporates and CSOs in India have largely operated in distinct spheres. "See, one has to understand that the corporate and the social sector have historically been two sides of the river. They've never really met."[50] Until this century, even when corporations engaged in CSR-type activities, it was usually philanthropy-oriented giving by a foundation rather than an operational partnership. This model kept the corporate offices and the CSO workers at arm's length even when the business was funding a CSO-run project. Most of the charitable giving by corporations, however, was channeled through their own foundations and consisted of donations to hospitals, schools, and temples.[51] The resulting lack of interaction or very rare

---

47 Personal Interview on Skype. April 20, 2018.
48 *CSR Journal*. 2014. "Resolve Tradition of Mistrust." *CSR Journal*. September 13. Available at https://thecsrjournal.in/tradition-of-mistrust-between-ngos-corporates-must-be-resolved/ (accessed June 6, 2022).
49 Nilsson, M. 2019. "Proximity and the trust formation process." *European Planning Studies*. 27(5), 841–861.
50 Arora, Deepak. 2015. Personal Interview with CEO of Essar Foundation, Mumbai, India.
51 Sundar, P. 2013. *Business & Community: The Story of Corporate Social Responsibility in India*. New Delhi: Sage Publications.

CORPORATIONS AND CIVIL SOCIETY ORGANIZATIONS 35

points of contact have led both the corporate world and the CSO sector to be quite suspicious of each other. Speaking of Indian corporations, one observer says, "They tend to see all CSOs as having bad reputations—that they are corrupt and don't do anything real. CSOs also have a negative perspective on corporations. They see them as thugs that have no clue about the real world and are basically just exploitative."[52] Corrupt and out of touch with reality are descriptors both types of organizations use about the other. Some of this suspicion is based on ignorance of each other, but not all of it.

In addition to the general lack of positive interaction in accounting for ill will, there is a long history of CSO mobilization in opposition to corporate operations. This is most well known in cases of land acquisition by big businesses or extractive mining industries where CSOs partner with local residents to block development. This has meant that in the cases when CSOs and corporations did interact in India, it was often as adversaries. Globally as well, "CSOs target corporations through boycotts, proxy campaigns, and other advocacy initiatives" in ways that can lead to corporations adopting defensive and reactive stances.[53] Actions against Coca-Cola, Pepsi, Vedanta, Tata Nano, and Maruti Suzuki are iconic instances of Indian CSOs, labor unions, and political parties coming together to resist attempts by large corporations to buy land and expand operations. This history of conflict and confrontation has fed into CSOs and corporations not trusting each other's motives and regarding partnerships with suspicion.

Can this history of mistrust and divergent visions of society be reconciled? The differences between these organizations can also be thought of as a kind of division of labor in which each one is fulfilling a different, but necessary social function. In that case, we can imagine some scenarios where CSOs and corporations may be able to take this division of labor and turn it into something productive for society as a whole. That is the thinking behind the Indian CSR law of 2013 which mandated corporate partnerships with CSOs. As the architect of the law put it,

There were five objectives for the CSR legislation. First we moved all CSR decisions to the board because that's where the best minds in the company are. Then the rules require that CSR activity be in the form of a project, not just a one-off publicity stunt. Now what happens when a corporate does a project? Well, they invest in planning the

---

52 Chatterjee, Bhaskar. 2019. Personal Interview, New Delhi, August 21.
53 Yaziji, M. and Doh, J. 2009. *CSOs and Corporations: Conflict and Collaboration*. Cambridge, UK: Cambridge University Press.

36   CORPORATE SOCIAL RESPONSIBILITY AND CIVIL SOCIETY

project, then they monitor how the project is being done and the money is spent. And finally they also develop ways to assess the outcomes and impact. See, companies are more efficient and they like to know what the impact is of the actions they are taking. Importantly this is a spending law. Not a promise to spend or allocate law. Spending. They must spend the money now, not make promises about the future and the pie in the sky things they will do one day. Companies are not designed to do CSR. So what does that mean? It means they have to outsource projects to CSOs and trusts. That was part of the design of the law. The trusts have expertise and knowledge that the companies need. So this can bridge the trust gap between corporates and civil society. Fifth we built a system for data collection and reporting. Basically, all the records of what the companies have spent and who has to be in the public domain. That way any researcher can compare what the company says it has done with the actual facts on the ground. This keeps the whole system accountable and is a key feature of India's CSR that is very academic friendly.[54]

There are some key ideas here that I explore in greater detail in Chapter 4. For now, we can see that the greater efficiency and impact orientation of corporations were meant to be joined with the expertise and knowledge of the people and issues that CSOs have to create synergy. That is, the design of CSO corporate collaborations is based upon these organizations having different strengths, which can make a greater impact than if they operate independently.

What is not acknowledged as clearly by Chatterjee is that not only do these organizations have different strengths, they also have different visions for India. While the corporation seeks to build a mass consumer society with enough investment in human capital to produce skilled workers, CSOs are much more oriented toward inclusion, justice, and other post-materialist values. This means that there are fundamental differences in goals and visions. It is possible that these differences can be put to productive work if CSOs could demand that corporations rethink business as usual. So instead of seeing the poor as an obstacle to overcome or as an undeveloped pool of consumers/workers, CSOs could encourage corporations to see the poor as partners, even stakeholders in society. And if corporations can encourage CSOs to think about sustainable models for their own operations, greater transparency, and accountability, that could

---

54 Chatterjee, Bhaskar. 2019. Personal Interview, New Delhi, August 21.

CORPORATIONS AND CIVIL SOCIETY ORGANIZATIONS 37

strengthen CSO impact. This hope that CSOs can teach corporations to truly engage in sustainable and inclusive development is at the heart of partnership models.

Before turning to emerging trends in the CSO–corporate relationship, it is important to take cognizance of some specifically Indian exceptions to the general model of a profit-maximizing company. Companies like Tata and Birla, inspired by a Gandhian trusteeship model offer another way of being successful businesses. M. K. Gandhi was the most prominent member of the Indian struggle for independence from the British. He believed that global capitalism was too large and impersonal to be a humane system. He often pointed out the excesses of capitalism but did not embrace socialism as many other Indian nationalists did. Instead, he offered the idea of trusteeship,[55] a concept that built on Carnegie's writing on philanthropy. Carnegie wrote, "Poor and restricted are our opportunities in this life; narrow our horizon; our best work most imperfect; but rich men should be thankful for one inestimable boon. They have it in their power during their lives to busy themselves in organizing benefactions from which the masses of their fellows will derive lasting advantage, and thus dignify their own lives."[56] That is, the wealthy have the opportunity to direct their talents to improving the lot of society and that is what their chief object must be.

Inspired by this, M. K. Gandhi suggested that rich industrialists should act as trustees of wealth—resources they hold and direct for the benefit of the many. "The emphasis is on transforming rather than demolishing the capitalist system. In essence, Gandhian trusteeship reposes faith in the capacity of individuals and entire classes to re-form themselves, on the premise that the capacity to seek redemption is intrinsic to human nature."[57] He calls on corporate leaders to engage in a spiritual practice of self-denial and service. In fact, "Trusteeship set a powerful trend in India's development trajectory that was articulated differently in different phases of its history, though, in conceptual terms, it has elements of Corporate Social Responsibility because the principle that the wealthy have a social

---

55 Bakshi, R. 2016. "Trusteeship: business and the economics of well-being." *Gateway House.* Available at https://www.gatewayhouse.in/wp-content/uploads/2016/09/FINALEdit_-Rajni_-Trusteeship_9March16-PDF.pdf (accessed June 20, 2022).

56 Carnegie, A. 1889. "The Gospel of Wealth." *North American Review.* Available at https://www.carnegie.org/publications/the-gospel-of-wealth/ (accessed June 20, 2022).

57 Bakshi, R. 2016. "Trusteeship: business and the economics of well-being." *Gateway House.* Available at https://www.gatewayhouse.in/wp-content/uploads/2016/09/FINALEdit_-Rajni_-Trusteeship_9March16-PDF.pdf (accessed June 20, 2022).

responsibility (whether institutionalized or not) remains as pivotal in Corporate Social Responsibility as it was true of Trusteeship."[58]

This model of Trusteeship attracted the men who led large family conglomerates like the Tatas and the Birlas. These industrialists made regular contributions to the freedom struggle, and while their companies stood to benefit from Indian independence, there is no doubt that they were personally moved by Gandhi's example and ideas. According to J. R. D. Tata, "He inspired in me, as in most people, a mixture of awe, admiration and affection combined with some scepticism[sic] about his economic philosophy despite which one would follow or support him to the end, come what may."[59] Even when they were not ready to adopt a Trustee model entirely, these corporate heads adopted CSR policies that reflected a deep commitment to giving back. Tata is well known for its exemplary integration of for-profit and nonprofit activities in India and globally.[60] This is an indigenous model of CSR that predates the emergence of this imperative in the West.

Contemporary Trends

The passage of 2013s Company Act that included Article 135 is the immediate basis for the transformation of the CSO–corporate relationship in India. It can be placed within a wider global trend in which these organizations are evolving their relationship. During the 1990s, university students in North America organized anti-sweatshop campaigns, which pushed a number of marquee brands like Nike and the Gap to adopt fair labor standards.[61] At the turn of the millennium, celebrities like Bono and George Clooney became prominent campaigners with CSO coalitions to work with states and corporations to address global poverty and human rights violations.[62] In contrast with the oppositional activism of the Seattle WTO protests in 1999, these campaigns were more reformist and offered corporations a path to redemption. Through partnerships with certifying agencies, the adoption

---

58 Chakrabarty, B. 2015. "Universal benefit: Gandhi's doctrine of trusteeship: A review article." *Modern Asian Studies*. 49(2), 572–608.

59 Sarkar, M. 2019. "Gandhi and the Tatas." *Tata Archives*. Available at https://www.tata.com/newsroom/heritage/gandhi-tatas-swaraj-to-satyagraha (accessed June 20, 2022).

60 Raianu, M. 2021. *Tata: The Global Corporation That Built Indian Capitalism*. Cambridge, MA: Harvard University Press.

61 A database on these efforts. Available at https://nvdatabase.swarthmore.edu/category/wave-campaigns/student-anti-sweatshop-labor-movement-1990s-2010s (accessed April 19, 2024).

62 Drezner, D. W. 2007. "Foreign Policy Goes Glam." *The National Interest*. 92, 22–28.

CORPORATIONS AND CIVIL SOCIETY ORGANIZATIONS 39

of industry best practices, and the UN Global Compact companies could place themselves on the moral side of history. Without having to abandon their core business practices, they could work with states and CSOs to adopt less harmful or even activist corporate social responsibility policies.

As the idea of private–public partnerships and the triple bottom line or ESG standards has evolved in recent decades, corporations are increasingly being included as potential reformers or even as core activists in movements to end the HIV epidemic or to promote gender equality or as environmentalists. While there are critiques of "greenwashing"—when a company spends more money advertising itself as eco-friendly than it does making its business processes environmentally sustainable[63]—or "pinkwashing"—in which support for LGBT rights is a way to hide state violence,[64] in international policy circles; there seems to be a consensus that businesses must be included in solutions, and not treated as external enemies. In a time when Walmart, Apple, and Amazon are operations that dwarf the economies of several countries, it is hard to imagine making progress on global problems without their cooperation.

As this book shows, when the state encourages cooperation between CSOs and corporations, in the aftermath of decades of hostility and opposition, the emerging partnerships are fraught. First, this move can be read as a way for the state to attempt to depoliticize disagreements over economic development. That is, by forcing CSOs and corporations to work together, the state denies that the visions for society offered by each of these organizations is mutually incompatible.[65] Then, rather than having to be the arbiter of competing visions—a battle that could be determined democratically, the state instead insists that the only differences are of means, not ends. That is, the partnership model suggests that CSOs and corporations share a consensus on what a successful national economy/society requires. They only disagree about how to get there. And that disagreement can be overcome, can even be productive, if only they actively engage one another and learn from each other. This is a kind of wishful thinking that is also dangerous because it is removing debate over the goals of economic development from the public democratic sphere and moving it into a technocratic and private arena.

---

63 Jahdi, Khosro S., and Acikdilli, G. 2009. "Marketing Communications and Corporate Social Responsibility (CSR): Marriage of Convenience or Shotgun Wedding?" *Journal of Business Ethics*. 88(1), 103–113.

64 Puar, Jasbir K. 2007. *Terrorist Assemblages: Homonationalism in Queer Times*. Durham: Duke University Press. p. 83.

65 Modi, N. 2019. "Address to the Nation." Available at https://www.news18.com/news/india/independence-day-full-text-of-narendra-modis-red-fort-speech-2271575.html (accessed June 19, 2022).

40   CORPORATE SOCIAL RESPONSIBILITY AND CIVIL SOCIETY

This is especially hazardous for CSOs which are almost always smaller, poorer, and less enmeshed with the state than their corporate partners. The main resource CSOs have is their reputation and their relationships with people. In partnerships, especially where those partnerships mostly consist of funding by corporations, the CSO is forced to adopt corporate practices of book-keeping, accounting, and assessment. Later chapters will explore more fully how what seem like neutral and bureaucratic practices actually have a great deal of power to reshape not just how CSOs operate internally, but also the work they do externally in the world. Today CSOs and corporations are working together more and more. The remainder of this book explores what consequences this is having for civil society and our ability to imagine collective futures.

Chapter 2

THE MATCHMAKER STATE

What role does the Indian state play in regulating commerce and the public sphere? All modern states provide basic services, regulate commerce, and promise the rule of law. In addition to these universal expectations, in India, the state also operates a number of public sector enterprises (PSEs) and tries to advance social reforms to promote equality among citizens. As such the Indian state has a particular agenda with regards to economic activity and civil society. In the next chapter, we see how the Indian state shifted its stance on the economy, moving from a command-and-control approach to one that regulates, and even supports private enterprise. Here, I provide a brief history of state-civil society relations in India covering the shift from contentious to cooperative relations in the colonial and post-colonial periods. The contemporary moment is one of the simultaneous embrace of *some* civil society organizations and the repression of others.

The history of state-civil society relations provides the context to understand the adoption of legislation that made CSR spending mandatory in 2013. This law (Article 135) is peculiar for a number of reasons, including its murky origins. The wording of the law forces a marriage between corporations and CSOs in which corporations have to spend a certain amount of money annually and CSOs have to act as implementing agencies to carry out their programs. This legislation reconciles the government's dual mandate for inclusive *and* rapid economic growth, but it was created in response to contingent processes of bureaucratic policymaking. This leads some to think the law is a symptom of neoliberal state withdrawal from the economy. I argue that although CSR is a way to reconcile the imperatives of supporting private enterprise and including the poor in economic gains, we should think of it as an extension of the state's control over the economy. That is, rather than the matchmaking state being used by hegemonic corporate interests, the state is attempting to reassert some control over them. Article 135 is an instance of the Indian state exerting power over business and civil society, not a state withdrawing from its responsibilities.

42   CORPORATE SOCIAL RESPONSIBILITY AND CIVIL SOCIETY

States: Origins and Functions

Max Weber provides a parsimonious definition of the state as a "human community that (successfully) claims the monopoly of the legitimate use of physical force within a given territory."[1] This draws attention to the function of the state in providing physical security through internal policing and the defense of the realm through armed forces.[2] The legitimacy of this use of force does a lot of work- indicating that the state must be an accepted "protection racket," not just one of many competitors.[3] In practical terms, it means that the state provides the rule of law and a regulatory framework for the population to engage in commerce. People move beyond simple barter economies when they can trust that contracts will be upheld by the state.[4] The rule of law can be thought of as one among many public goods the minimal state provides.

A lively literature takes Eurocentric accounts of state creation to task. These critical scholars argue that state formation has looked quite different depending on location. Geography is a key variable in shaping the types of governing structures that emerge as it influences the sources of production and these in turn constrain the possibilities for wealth accumulation. The density of population and linguistic diversity are also found to be important factors that shape governing structures.[5] In many cases, people have escaped nascent states in order to not be governed. That is, historically many people have opted out of the state project. Today that option has all but disappeared. The modern Indian state includes people who have been subject to centralized authority for ages as well as those who had previously escaped it by moving into forests and hills. Much of the "internal colonialism" directed at the Northeastern states and Kashmir can be understood as an attempt by the state-centric plains people to assert their authority over populations that seek to evade it.[6]

---

1 Weber, Max. 1918. *Politics as a Vocation.* Reprint Indianapolis, IN: Hackett Publishing 2004.

2 Tilly, Charles. 1992. *Coercion, Capital, and European States.* Cambridge, MA: Blackwell.

3 Nozick, R. 1974. *Anarchy, Sate, and Utopia.* New York: Basic Books.

4 Bates, Robert. 2001. *Prosperity and Violence: The Political Economy of Development.* New York, NY: Norton; North, Douglass and Barry Weingast. 1989. "Constitutions and Commitments." *Journal of Economic History.* 59(4).

5 Herbst, J. 1990. "War and the State in Africa." *International Security.* 14(4), 117–139; Taylor, B., and R. Botea. 2008. "Tilly Tally: War-Making and State-Making in the Contemporary Third World." *International Studies Review.* 10(1), 27–56.

6 Scott, James C. 2009. *The Art of Not Being Governed.* New Haven, CT: Yale University Press.

THE MATCHMAKER STATE 43

Public goods are those goods (such as clean air) that are non-excludable and therefore pose particular collective action problems. That is, in order to have public goods some people have to take on costly actions, but they cannot reserve the fruits of that action only to themselves. For example, once factory owners have limited their emissions, the cleaner air belongs to anyone who breathes. This means that a society must create incentives to get factory owners to take on the costs of less polluting production methods. The structuring and enforcing of incentives (or sanctions) is typically done by the state, which in an ideal sense, can step in to create trust so that common resources and public goods can be enjoyed by all.[7] Another, darker, view of this role of the state is that it promises to offer public goods as a way of further extracting productive value from its people.[8] That is, the governing practices of the state are simply ways to more deeply ensnare the population in its projects of producing surplus capital.

Over time most states have expanded their scope to also provide services such as health care, education, support for the indigent, and labor rights. Two processes have shaped the expansion of state services in most societies. The first has been a secularization of welfare whereby support for the poor and sick has moved from the responsibility of kin groups and religious authorities to the state. As the state has taken on more authority over people's lives, it has also found itself providing them with greater support.[9] The second important process is the industrialization of the economy. Those states which industrialized later generally have done so with greater state involvement in the process.[10] A critical aspect of this has been the use of schools to create disciplined workers and to impart a national identity to the people.[11] Nation building depends on particular forms of economic development and economic growth depends on nation building.

---

7 Ostrom, Elinor. 2009. "Beyond Markets and States: Polycentric governance of complex economic systems" Nobel Prize Lecture December 8 Available at https://www.nobelprize.org/uploads/2018/06/ostrom_lecture.pdf (accessed June 2, 2020).

8 Foucault, Michel. 1975. *Discipline and Punish*. Reprint New York, NY: Vintage Books 1995.

9 Gill, A., and E. Lundsgaarde. 2004. State Welfare Spending and Religiosity: A Cross-National Analysis. *Rationality and Society*. 16(4), 399–436; Kahl, S. 2005. The Religious Roots of Modern Poverty Policy: Catholic, Lutheran, and Reformed Protestant Traditions Compared. *European Journal of Sociology*, 46(1), 91–126.

10 Gershenkron, Alexander. 1962. *Economic Backwardness in Historical Perspective*. Cambridge, MA: Belknap Press.

11 Gellner, Ernest. 1983. *Nations and Nationalism*. Oxford, UK: Blackwell; Hobsbawm, Eric. 1990. *Nations and Nationalism Since 1780*. Cambridge, UK: Cambridge University Press.

44   CORPORATE SOCIAL RESPONSIBILITY AND CIVIL SOCIETY

Post-colonial states are typically latecomers to industrialization and also to the creation of national identities. Metropolitan authorities shaped their colonial economies to be the source of raw materials and actively worked to undermine the emergence of unified political identities.[12] This meant that at independence these countries, including India, used the state to shape the economy and from their inception, they committed to the provision of a wide range of public services to their people as a purposeful contrast with the colonial state.[13] The promises made to provide services often outstrip the actual ability of the state to marshal and distribute resources in an effective manner. This has led to the argument that states with weak capacity but wide scope, are likely to become failed states.[14] Consequently, the neoliberal prescription for this problem is to have states with strong capacity and limited scope. Such a neoliberal state would have a strong security apparatus but provide minimal social services. Nonetheless, the expectation in a country like India is that the government will play an active role in regulating commerce *and* engaging with civil society. This means that the Indian state owns and operates a number of public sector enterprises (PSEs) that produce a variety of goods. It also means that the state acts as a vanguard in promoting social change and nation building.

The Indian state, founded in 1947, set itself an ambitious agenda. It promised not only to grant its people civil and political rights but also; to reduce inequality, promote justice, protect labor, advance gender equality, invest in agriculture and industry, and contribute to world peace.[15] In this sense, B. R. Ambedkar's leadership in drafting the Indian constitution is highly significant in shaping its wide commitments.[16] He was anti-capitalist, a fierce critic of Hindu prejudices, and a firm believer in the role of the state as an engine for social reform.[17] Along with Jawaharlal Nehru, Ambedkar

---

12 Chatterjee, Partha. 1993. *The Nation and its Fragments.* Princeton, NJ: Princeton University Press.

13 Arndt, H. W. 1987. *Economic Development.* Chicago, IL: Chicago University Press; Getachew, Adom. 2018. *World Making After Empire: The Rise and Fall of Self-Determination.* Princeton, NJ: Princeton University Press.

14 Fukuyama, F. 2004. The Imperative of State-Building. *Journal of Democracy.* 15(2), 17–31.

15 Indian Constitution. 1950. "Directive Principles" Available at https://www.mea.gov.in/Images/pdf1/Part4.pdf (accessed June 7, 2020).

16 Rathore, Aakash. 2020. *Ambedkar's Preamble: A Secret History of the Constitution of India.* New Delhi: Penguin. 17 Omvedt, Gail. 2004. *Ambedkar: Towards an Enlightened India.* New Delhi: Penguin.

17 Omvedt, Gail. 2004. *Ambedkar: Towards an Enlightened India.* New Delhi: Penguin Random House.

THE MATCHMAKER STATE

45

gave shape to a vision for an independent Indian state that called it to lead the way in reforming economic and social life—most notably by abolishing the practice of untouchability.

The Soviet Union's rapid industrialization inspired the creation of an Indian Planning Commission with five-year plans for economic development.[18] The government nationalized and founded a number of publicly owned firms to produce everything from electricity to cigarettes while it also invested heavily in technical higher education. In its early years, the state initiated some land reforms and made revisions to the personal laws that applied to Hindu families to make them less sexist.[19] Both of these efforts met with organized and sustained resistance. Eventually, the state accepted very partial land reforms but gradually ground down the opposition to the reforms of the Hindu code by breaking the reforms into smaller pieces of legislation over a few years. People expected the government to be active in the political, economic, and social spheres—a very wide scope for a new state. While the next chapter discusses the changes in the role played by the state in the economy over the past seventy years, this next section discusses the evolution of the state's relationship to civil society.

State and Civil Society in India

Civil society played an important *political* role in the colonial period. Because the British authorities restricted the space for Indians to engage in politics, religious organizations, and literary societies were the foundation of Indian civil society.[20] They engaged in welfare provision but also became sites for articulating a nationalist imagination. In these societies, educated elite men (and some women) gathered to construct a story of India and in doing so they debated various visions for Indian society. These debates fed into the anti-colonial mobilization of the 1920s onwards, where under Gandhi's leadership the masses became politically active.[21] Civic life had two orientations: social reform through charitable works and nation

---

18 Frankel, Francine. 2005. *India's Political Economy*, 2nd Edition. New Delhi: Oxford University Press.
19 On land reforms see Varshney, Ashutosh. 1998. "India Defies the Odds: Why Democracy Survives." *Journal of Democracy.* 9(3), 36–50 and on reforms of the Hindu code see Williams, Rina Verma. 2006 *Postcolonial Politics and Personal Laws.* New Delhi: Oxford University Press.
20 Bose, Sugata and Ayesha Jalal. 1998. *Modern South Asia.* London: Routledge.
21 Chatterjee, Partha. 2004 *The Politics of the Governed.* New York, NY: Columbia University Press.

46   CORPORATE SOCIAL RESPONSIBILITY AND CIVIL SOCIETY

making through a range of protest campaigns. The non-democratic nature of the state meant that civil society organizations largely took on a confrontational approach to the state. They worked in competition with it by providing education and uplift services to groups it failed to serve. And they confronted it openly as they sought self-determination for Indians. One of the key features that underpins India's democracy is the role that peaceful mass mobilization played in achieving political independence.[22] The Indian state was not born from armed struggle but through popular protest and elite negotiation.

Post-independence, civil society became much less significant as a check on the power of the state. Instead, many of the leaders of civic organizations joined forces with the government, or even became members of the government, in order to engage in nation-building. Annie Devenish in her history of the Indian women's movement documents how many of the leaders of women's organizations moved into roles within the government.[23] They thought that the post-colonial state would work for the people and that the best way to serve was by joining the state. At this time, the boundary between the state and civil society blurred and this period until the late 1960s was a time of extensive cooperation between the two. An excellent example of this is the way the state supported the creation of self-help groups (SHGs) among rural women—a model made famous later in the 1980s as microfinance for women. These groups were given organizational support and funds by the government, the extension workers were women who had been active in women's organizations, and the SHGs themselves became forms of grassroots civil society. Should these SHGs be considered part of civil society or extensions of the state?

During the 1970s, it became apparent the state was falling well short of any expectation held by civic activists that it could serve as a benign and robust guardian of the people. Instead, activists realized that the state was failing to advance the well-being of the people, especially the historically marginalized (women, Dalits, Adivasis). As the government under Indira Gandhi centralized power, and in 1975, suspended political and civil rights, the divide between the state and civil society reemerged. The mobilizations that prompted the 1975–1977 Emergency saw coalitions of Gandhian activists, environmentalists, feminists, but also right-wing religious nationalists uniting in opposition to the state. Civil society once again became

---

22 Varshney, Ashutosh. 1998. "India Defies the Odds: Why Democracy Survives." *Journal of Democracy*. 9(3), 36–50.

23 Devenish, Annie. 2019. *Debating Women's Citizenship in India 1930–1960*. New Delhi: Bloomsbury.

THE MATCHMAKER STATE   47

a site for explicit political activism in opposition to state policies.[24] When a coalition government replaced the Congress in 1977, it briefly introduced funding to support CSOs in providing services to the people. But this coalition government fell apart and the Congress returned to power, once again creating a rift between the government and civil society.

During the following decades, the international environment became very supportive of CSOs. When the Soviet Union disintegrated and Eastern Europe democratized, civil society was seen as the lynchpin for the mobilizations that ended the Cold War. In a rush to introduce democracy and market capitalism to formerly communist countries, the World Bank and other multilateral institutions embraced civil society. They saw it as a more efficient and bottom-up way to transform societies. And in their embrace, they prescribed new roles for CSOs all over the world.[25] The number of development CSOs in India grew at a rapid pace in the 1990s and 2000s in response to new funding opportunities at the international level. In addition, the international support for CSOs and participatory approaches to development encouraged the Indian government to create more spaces for civil society inclusion in development programs. Along with steps to boost local government through *panchayats*, or village councils, and decentralizing power to the states, the Rajiv Gandhi government rapidly increased development funds for CSO service delivery.

In the 1990s, civil society moved from protecting its autonomy from political parties to becoming partners with the state in service delivery. As multilateral aid was directed to India with provisions for the inclusion of CSOs, more and more groups became "implementing agencies" for state welfare schemes. Advocacy and rights-based groups became distant from the service provider CSOs and had to search for nongovernment support. Many of them became dependent on international foundations and Northern CSOs to cover their operating costs. The search for grant funds shaped CSO priorities and left them open to the charge of being foreign puppets, even when they were acting independently. The professionalization of advocacy work and close cooperation with the state by grassroots agencies combined to create a less radical and less oppositional civil society.[26]

This shift to a more cooperative model did not make civil society ineffective at driving social change, but it did limit their horizons.[27] In 2004,

---

24 Deo, N. 2018. *Mobilizing Religion and Gender in India*. London: Routledge.
25 Chandhoke, N. 2003. *The Conceits of Civil Society*. New Delhi: Oxford University Press.
26 Deo, N. and D. McDuie Ra. 2012. *The Politics of Collective Advocacy in India*. New York: Kumarian.
27 Chandhoke, N. 2012. "Whatever Happened to Civil Society?" *Economic and Political Weekly*. 47(3), June 9.

48   CORPORATE SOCIAL RESPONSIBILITY AND CIVIL SOCIETY

a Congress-led coalition came to power. While Manmohan Singh—the architect of India's economic liberalization—served as Prime Minister, the power behind the throne was held by Sonia Gandhi. She created a National Advisory Council which included a number of civil society stalwarts. Singh continued moving India toward a neoliberal economic model with the state supporting big business growth while Gandhi and the NAC adopted plans and policies to help the poorest Indians. This expansion of the welfare state included the Right to Information Act, the Right to Education, the MNREGA employment guarantee, and so on.[28] Each of these new rights were demanded by grassroots social movements that collaborated with the members of the NAC. During this time period, civil society leaders considered themselves quite successful.[29] It is in only in hindsight that some look back on this time and see it as also a series of missed opportunities. According to one of the key architects of the civil society-NAC collaboration and leader of Wada Na Todo Abhiyan,

> It was a completely schizophrenic existence we had. So that government was clearly on the one hand Sonia Gandhi [party chief and pro-welfare] and on the other hand Montek, Manmohan, Chidambaram [economists and pro-privatization] so that's how it worked [...] See ultimately in politics you don't win all and that was the assessment we were making. We were able to get the 'right to information', the 'right to education' eventually even the 'right to food' which for years the Manmohan camp was very, very reluctant but we got the 'right to food' also the 'forest rights act' [was a] phenomenal win. So many wins then you feel that okay. But yes, you are right, as in there were huge issues as in Congress revised the FCRA[30] and we are now paying for it. Obviously in the hindsight it's easy to say. But I started with this admission that I think we made that mistake [...]. Can you really collaborate with power and then say that we will be able to influence [it]? So that's the whole thing and while doing all that, that's the question, right? And in doing all that we lost our own ability to mobilize people.[31]

---

28 These are all progressive pieces of legislation that expanded the social and economic rights of Indian citizens to secure their lives and livelihoods.

29 Behar, A and R. Singh. 2018. "India Civil Society: Beyond the Cooperation-Competition Binary." In *Government- CSO Relationships in Africa, Asia, Europe, and MENA* edited by R. Marchetti, London: Routledge.

30 The Foreign Contributions Regulation Act (FCRA) governs the rules by which CSOs can receive foreign funding and is discussed below.

31 Behar, Amitabh. 2019 Personal interview September 26 New Delhi.

THE MATCHMAKER STATE

This activist identifies the close collaboration between civil society and the state as productive but also flawed. During their embrace of the UPA[32] government, civic activists missed the chance to prevent the passage of a series of regulations that have led to closer regulation (and therefore control over) CSOs. They also failed to join in the mobilization against corruption that was led by Anna Hazare.[33] As a result many of these groups seemed to be partisans of the Congress party which made it easier for the subsequent BJP government to freeze them out of policymaking.

Not everyone shares these regrets. Another eminent activist and scholar— Mihir Shah—defends the National Advisory Council.[34] "The body achieved a lot. The rights-based legislation were unprecedented in the country's history [...] these cannot be reversed." He believes that civil society must remain flexible—working with the state when it allows collaboration, stepping aside when it won't, and even being willing to confront it when appropriate. He argues that the opportunity for civil society activists to influence the state is so valuable that they should be willing to sacrifice some of their "purity" in order to be seen as acceptable partners of the state. Finally, he points out that there are many committed bureaucrats within the government, and we should not simplistically paint the state and civil society as mutually exclusive or antagonistic.[35]

Regulating Civil Society Today

The first United Progressive Alliance (UPA) government from 2004 to 2009 was generally supportive of civil society, and through the NAC it expanded the space for civil society to act. But, the second term of the UPA led to greater restriction of civil society space through increased regulation and investigations. The most significant of these were the revisions to the Foreign Contributions Regulation Act (FCRA) by the Home Ministry in 2010.[36]

---

32 The United Progressive Alliance (UPA) was the name of a Congress party led coalition that contested elections together. Until 2014, no party had won enough votes to rule India alone since 1989. The BJP led coalition was called the National Democratic Alliance (NDA).

33 Behar, A and R. Singh. 2018. "India Civil Society: Beyond the Cooperation-Competition Binary." In *Government- CSO Relationships in Africa, Asia, Europe, and MENA* edited by R. Marchetti, London: Routledge.

34 For a discussion of these rights based laws see *Times of India* 2014. "NAC pats itself for historic laws." May 7 New Delhi.

35 Shah, Mihir. 2019. Personal Interview July 20 Kochi, Kerala.

36 India Development Review. 2019. "IDR Explains: FCRA *India Development Review* Available at https://idronline.org/idr-explains-fcra/ (accessed July 20, 2020).

50 CORPORATE SOCIAL RESPONSIBILITY AND CIVIL SOCIETY

This law was first introduced in 1976 by the Indira Gandhi government to prevent foreign interference in Indian politics. Under the law, political parties, newspapers and civil servants were banned from accepting foreign funding and CSOs were required to report any such funding to the government. In 1984, the law was modified to require CSOs to receive prior approval before they could begin to accept foreign donations. This law was one of the regulations that made cooperation between CSOs and political parties harder because CSOs that were seen as being close to political parties were denied FCRA clearance. It also meant that foreign funding could only go to organizations that were institutionalized (they had to have been functioning for at least 3 years and there was a minimum amount of funding they had to receive) which left smaller community-based organizations out of the ambit of foreign aid.

In 2010, the UPA government issued new FCRA rules according to which CSOs not only had to report their foreign income annually, but also had to reapply for their FCRA clearances every five years. It also restricted the amount of administrative costs that could be covered by foreign funding to 50%, which is a way of reducing the possibility of advocacy by groups that are largely funded by foreigners. Instead, the groups have to engage in service delivery and raise some of their funds domestically.

There are now about 21,000 nonprofits registered under the FCRA rules. Many groups have had their clearances revoked for failure to file their annual reports in a timely fashion.[37] Since 2014, about 18,000 CSOs have been removed from the FCRA roster.[38] Most of them were removed for failing to file their paperwork correctly, many because they no longer are operational, but some because they have been targeted by the state for engaging in political opposition to the ruling government.[39] The most recent modifications to the FCRA rules now require *all* the office holders of the CSO to file affidavits

---

37 Hindustan Times. 2019. "FCRA licence of over 4,800 CSOs cancelled in 3 years: Govt tells Rajya Sabha." Available at https://www.hindustantimes.com/india-news/fcra-licence-of-over-4-800-CSOs-cancelled-in-3-years-govt-tells-rajya-sabha/story-wXsgRl7pjk7xxWGyA083QO.html (accessed July 20, 2020).

38 Hindustan Times. 2019 "Government tightens religious conversion rule for CSOs in foreign funding tweaks" September 17 Available at https://www.hindustantimes.com/india-news/no-need-to-declare-foreign-gifts-up-to-rs-ll/story-IO2BATHICu92LFblZyY0iN.html (accessed July 20, 2020).

39 Nayak, V. 2016. "FCRA and CSOs: What lies behind the government's crackdown?" *The Wire* video interview Available at https://www.youtube.com/watch?v=i0zpK605bxI (accessed July 20, 2020).

THE MATCHMAKER STATE   51

to attest that they have not been involved in any religious conversions or seditious activity.[40] The tightening of restrictions narrows the operating space for CSOs that serve Christian and Muslim communities in particular. The FCRA and its evolution is a key means by which the state seeks to control the work of CSOs. While the Modi government has used the law to target its critics, the revision of the law was initiated under the UPA government.

Another significant step in chilling civil society initiated by the UPA, but which came to fruition under the BJP government, was a report by the Intelligence Bureau into antidevelopment advocacy by CSOs. The report estimated that CSOs gathering information and engaging in advocacy could be slowing GDP growth by 2–3% annually.[41] How did the IB come to this conclusion? They explain that, "These foreign donors lead local CSOs to provide field reports which are used to build a record against India and serve as tools for the strategic foreign policy interests of the Western government[s]. All the above is used to build a record against a country or an individual in order to keep the entity under pressure and under a state of under-development." The Intelligence Bureau suggests that donors, "in the US, the UK, Germany, The Netherlands and Scandinavian countries" use Indian organizations to collect damning data on various development projects and then use these reports to slow or stop the projects.[42] They point to international and grassroots mobilizations against nuclear power plants, mining projects, and hydroelectric plants—all of which have significant negative impacts on local populations—as examples of stalled development. They further imply that the intent of these mobilizations is not sustainable development, or the rights of marginalized groups, but rather to keep India under-developed and weak in the international Great Game.

This report was leaked within weeks of the NDA government taking over and set the tone for how the state viewed those parts of civil society that operate under human rights and environmental sustainability agendas. These sections of civil society, because they pose roadblocks to massive extractive industry, are

---

40 Tripathi, R. 2019. "Each NGO Member Will Have To Declare No Association with Religious Conversion" *The Economic Times* September 17. Available at https://www. deccanchronicle.com/nation/current-affairs/170919/govts-new-rule-ngo-staff-need-to-declare-no-role-in-conversions.html (accessed May 9, 2024).

41 Ranjan, A. 2014. "Foreign CSOs are actively stalling development." *The Indian Express* June 7. Available at https://indianexpress.com/article/india/india-others/foreign-aided-ngos-are-actively-stalling-development-ib-tells-pmo-in-a-report/ (accessed May 9, 2024).

42 Intelligence Bureau, Ministry of Home Affairs. 2014. *Impact of CSOs on Development.* June 3 (IR/IS 002) Available at https://archive.nyu.edu/bitstream/2451/40704/2/NGO%20report.pdf (accessed May 9, 2024).

framed as antidevelopment. And because the primary job of the Indian state is seen as the promotion of economic development, these CSOs are branded anti-national.[43] Somehow those who call for the protection of marginalized people and conserving the natural habitat are portrayed as threats to India.[44] A shocking example of this has been the arrest of 22-year-old Disha Ravi for sharing a Google Document with Greta Thunberg in support of the farmer's mobilization of 2021. Her crime was framed as advocating a war against India when in fact it was a set of talking points commonly used in activist circles to frame and mobilize support.[45]

While the FCRA crackdowns and the discourse surrounding anti-development CSOs can give the impression that civic space in India has been continuously constricted since the BJP came to power in 2014, in fact the state is increasing support to certain other civic organizations. Groups affiliated with the BJP in the Sangh Parivar (family of organizations) who all subscribe to the ideology of Hindutva are being supported by the state. In some cases, this means that groups engaging in extrajudicial violence are granted immunity and their members are allowed to act as vigilantes. These vigilantes are most notorious for their enforcement of "beef bans."

The sale and consumption of beef is restricted in 24 of 29 states in India, and 15 states have total bans on the slaughter of cattle.[46] After the Modi government came to power, vigilantes calling themselves *gau rakshaks* (cow protectors) assaulted and even killed individuals accused of violating these bans.[47] Being able to engage in violence with the connivance of the state is not the kind of patronage we usually associate with civil society, but in the case of India, this non-application of criminal and civil law is an important form of

---

43 Mohanty, Ranjita. 2020. Personal Interview. July 20 Kochi, Kerala.

44 Bornstein, E. and A. Sharma. 2016. "The Righteous and the Rightful: The Technomoral Politics of CSOs, Social Movements, and the State in India." *American Ethnologist.* 43, 76–90.

45 Delhi Police. 2021. https://twitter.com/DelhiPolice/status/1360913823515901964?s=20 (accessed June 7, 2021). and Misra, Tanvi. 2021. "Indian Climate Activist Disha Ravi Arrested, Caught in India's Sedition Dragnet." *Teen Vogue.* February 20. (accessed June 7, 2021).

46 Dutta, S. 2015. "Where you can and can't eat beef in India." *Wall Street Journal.* August 6. Available at https://blogs.wsj.com/indiarealtime/2015/08/06/where-you-can-and-cant-eat-beef-in-india/#:~:text=Overall%2C%2024%20of%20India's%20 29,of%20cows%20and%20other%20cattle (accessed July 24, 2020).

47 Human Rights Watch. 2019. "Vigilante 'Cow Protection' Groups Attack Minorities." February 18 Available at https://www.hrw.org/news/2019/02/19/india-vigilante-cow-protection-groups-attack-minorities# (accessed June 29, 2021).

THE MATCHMAKER STATE

support for Hindu nationalist groups. Recognizing the complex relationship between civil society and violence remains unusual in civil society literature despite there being significant historical evidence that these are not mutually exclusive phenomena.[48]

In addition to this, organizations that espouse Hindutva ideology have access to more funding, the patronage of public authorities, and are less likely to be targeted for the enforcement of the rules used to repress other civic organizations. The latter is very significant because the legal regulation of CSOs, especially those engaged in advocacy work, is highly subjective and can be quite extensive.[49] Legally CSOs are prohibited from political advocacy, which not only proscribes their support for a particular candidate or party, but also disallows advocacy for legal changes or policy adoption. Most of the time these rules are applied narrowly, but in some cases, they have been used to target CSOs that advocate for people/positions that the government doesn't like. Examples include crackdowns on the Lawyers Collective and Teesta Setalvad—both cases in which the activists were resisting the government in the courts.

Another way in which the state expands space for select types of civil society organizations while simultaneously restricting it for others is through its creation of a bureaucracy for civil society. The 2014 Modi government abolished the Planning Commission and replaced it with the Niti Ayog to be the source of ideas for economic policies. The Niti Ayog created an online portal for CSOs to register themselves in the hopes of becoming more connected to government funding opportunities and private–public partnerships. "VOs/CSOs play a major role in the development of the nation by supplementing the efforts of the Government. This portal enables VOs/CSOs to enrol [sic] centrally and thus facilitates creation of a repository of information about VOs/CSOs, Sector/State wise."[50] According to the website, 97,237 voluntary organizations/nongovernmental organizations have enrolled in the portal. It also lists 89 CSOs that are on a "blacklist". No further information about this blacklist is provided. Those organizations that wish to contract with the government have to register on this portal

---

48 Dorner, W. and R. A. List. 2012. *Civil Society, Conflict and Violence.* London, UK: Bloomsbury Press.
49 Civic Freedom Monitor. 2020. *India.* Available at https://www.icnl.org/resources/civic-freedom-monitor/india (accessed August 7, 2020).
50 Niti Ayog. 2020. "CSO Darpan" Available at https://ngodarpan.gov.in/index.php/home/blacklisted (accessed May 9, 2024).

and provide information about their activities. This requirement calls for a high level of bureaucratic and technological literacy, which excludes many community-based organizations that are run by marginalized groups themselves. Thus, even when the state seeks to collaborate with civil society groups, its methods themselves create insiders and outsiders. Nonetheless, this portal and the funding partnerships it promises are another example of the way the state under the BJP is in fact supporting *some* civil society organizations.

To conclude this section, I have shown that the relationship between the state and civil society has evolved over time. Many of the restrictions on civil society that are seen today were initiated by the Congress led government and honed as cudgels by the BJP in subsequent years. The heavy regulation of civil society creates spaces for some groups to face less monitoring and others to receive state support—thus creating passive and active forms of state-civil society collaboration. I also have argued that the Indian state has a commitment to economic development and that this is often imbued with nationalist ideology. Therefore, threats to the chosen model of economic growth are interpreted as anti-national and subject to repression. Thus, a number of CSOs who advocate for the poor and marginalized find themselves as enemies of the state. This is the context needed to understand how Article 135, mandating corporate social responsibility spending, is in reality about the state exerting control over the market and civil society rather than a withdrawal from the arena of sustainable development.

Table Corporate Social Responsibility Over Time

Time period	Economic currents	State role	Corporate CSR
1850–1914	Industrialization	Colonial, extraction	Dynastic charity
1914–1947	Trade barriers for new industries	Colonial, exploitative	Support freedom struggle
1947–1960	Socialism, protectionism	Five-year plans	Support new state; launch own rural initiatives
1960–1990	Heavy regulations	License raj; development failures	Corporate trusts
1991–2013	Liberalization	Shrinking in production; expanding in social provision	Family trusts, private-public partnerships, NGO sponsorship
2013–present	Globalization	Need to manage inequality	Introduction of mandatory 2% rule in Article 135

THE MATCHMAKER STATE   55

Four Stories about Article 135

(1) Every company having a net worth of rupees five hundred crores or more, or turnover of rupees one thousand crores or more or a net profit of rupees five crores or more during any financial year shall constitute a Corporate Social Responsibility Committee of the Board consisting of three or more directors, out of which at least one director shall be an independent director.

(2) The Board's report under subsection (3) of section 134 shall disclose the composition of the Corporate Social Responsibility Committee.

(3) The Corporate Social Responsibility Committee shall—(a) formulate and recommend to the Board, a Corporate Social Responsibility Policy which shall indicate the activities to be undertaken by the company as specified in Schedule VII; (b) recommend the amount of expenditure to be incurred on the activities referred to in clause (a); and (c) monitor the Corporate Social Responsibility Policy of the company from time to time.

(4) The Board of every company referred to in subsection (1) shall— (a) after taking into account the recommendations made by the Corporate Social Responsibility Committee, approve the Corporate Social Responsibility Policy for the company and disclose contents of such Policy in its report and also place it on the company's website, if any, in such manner as may be prescribed; and (b) ensure that the activities as are included in Corporate Social Responsibility Policy of the company are undertaken by the company.

(5) The Board of every company referred to in subsection (1), shall ensure that the company spends, in every financial year, at least two percent. of the average net profits of the company made during the three immediately preceding financial years, in pursuance of its Corporate Social Responsibility Policy: Provided that the company shall give preference to the local area and areas around it where it operates, for spending the amount earmarked for Corporate Social Responsibility activities: Provided further that if the company fails to spend such amount, the Board shall, in its report made under clause (o) of subsection (3) of section 134, specify the reasons for not spending the amount. *Explanation.—* For the purposes of this section "average net profit" shall be calculated in accordance with the provisions of section 198.[51]

---

51 Ministry of Corporate Affairs, Government of India Available at https://www.mca. gov.in/SearchableActs/Section135.htm (accessed November 5, 2020).

56   CORPORATE SOCIAL RESPONSIBILITY AND CIVIL SOCIETY

In the introduction to this book, I shared the puzzle that this law was passed even in the absence of a specific group interested in its adoption. In 2009, the Corporate Affairs Ministry first introduced the idea of the two percent spending on CSR but faced immediate opposition. It relented and made the provision voluntary for the private sector but mandatory for the public sector. Large public-owned enterprises have been required to follow this practice for some time. Minister Murli Deora explained the motivation for the law. "It is quite surprising that they (companies) do not spend even half a percent of their profit in social welfare, but they forget that a prosperous society is a must for their own survival." He went on to say he "wanted companies to help in bridging the wide gap between the rich and the poor and the party also wants companies to take their social responsibilities seriously."[52] When I asked people in the CSR world how the law came to pass, I heard four stories. They are (1) the neoliberalism story, (2) the foreign aid story, (3) the caste story, and (4) the bureaucracy story. It is useful to differentiate between the functions that CSR may play in India at the current juncture from the question of how an unpopular idea was adopted as a mandatory law. The functions it fulfills help explain the rapid acceptance and implementation of the law, but they don't explain its initial drafting or adoption. First, I present the stories circulating about this law. Then this chapter concludes by suggesting how to interpret them to best understand the origins and subsequent reception of Article 135.

Neoliberalism Story

Within the framework of India's adoption of neoliberalism, the Congress government needed a way to look like it cared about the poor without making any meaningful changes in the way the economy worked. The party manifesto leading up to the 2009 elections stated, "The Indian National Congress seeks a fresh mandate on the basis of its core values and ideology—secularism, nationalism, social justice, and economic growth for all, especially for the *aam admi*."[53] On economic policy the Congress tried to straddle the path of maximizing fast growth through support for big business through

---

52 Jayaswal, Rajeev. 2011. "Murli Deora Favours Mandatory CSR." *Economic Times* May 23. Available at. https://economictimes.indiatimes.com/news/company/corporate-trends/murli-deora-favours-mandatory-corporate-social-responsibility/articleshow/8519583.cms (accessed December 2023).

53 Indian National Congress Manifesto 2009. Available at http://www.indiaenvironmentportal.org.in/files/Congress%20Manifesto.pdf (accessed May 9, 2024).

THE MATCHMAKER STATE 57

deregulation while also attempting to be inclusive toward the *aam admi*, or common man, through further extension of various welfare schemes.

In their 2009 manifesto, the emphasis was on macroeconomic policies that would stimulate business activity. The creation of the MGNREGA national work scheme (Mahatma Gandhi National Rural Employment Guarantee Act) was the major policy achievement that they touted as a nod to the need to make growth work for poor Indians. One commentator wrote that their, "commitment to inclusiveness is a façade that attracts the *aam admi*, but obscures the ugly reality- India is on track to become another oligarchy [...]."[54] Others suggest that CSR is the ultimate manifestation of neoliberalism as corporates take over the state's welfare functions in ways that ultimately boost their bottom line.[55] Arundhati Roy describes the philanthropic foundations set up by business houses, "Non-tax-paying legal entities with massive resources and an almost unlimited brief—wholly unaccountable, wholly nontransparent— what better way to parlay economic wealth into political, social, and cultural capital, to turn money into power? What better way for usurers to use a minuscule percentage of their profits to run the world?"[56] This view is in keeping with the wider diagnosis offered by Atul Kohli, who argues that "the pro-business tilt of the Indian state is responsible both for the progressive dynamism at the apex and for the failure to include India's numerous excluded groups in the polity and the economy."[57] That is, rapid economic growth in certain industries has failed to lead to substantial improvements in human development because the state is beholden to large businesses. Article 135 is an attempt by business and the state to hide their collusion and to present a kinder face to the people at very little cost.

While this story is compelling and can make its narrator seem worldly wise, it is belied by the evidence of strong opposition to the passage of 135 by the business community. In 2011, Montek Singh Ahluwalia, as Deputy Chair of the Planning Commission, declared his opposition to the idea that Indian businesses should be required to set aside two percent of their annual profits for CSR funding. He said, "If you want them to spend

---

54 Chandra, N. 2010. Inclusive Growth in Neoliberal India: A Facade? *Economic and Political Weekly.* 45(8), 43–56.

55 Nandy, Mrittika. 2015. "Taming Inequalities: Neoliberalism and CSR in the Indian context." *Journal of General Management Research.* 2(2), 40–49 and Rana, Subir. 2015. "CSR as the New Age Corporate Practice: Reality, Issues, and its Impact on Workers in the Field." *Asian Labour Review.* 1, 115–124.

56 Roy, Arundhati. 2014. *Capitalism: A Ghost Story.* Haymarket Books: Chicago, IL.

57 Kohli, Atul. 2012. *Poverty Amid Plenty in the New India.* Cambridge, UK: Cambridge University Press.

58   CORPORATE SOCIAL RESPONSIBILITY AND CIVIL SOCIETY

another two percent, that's like saying that corporate tax would be raised to 32 percent. It's better to do that. You cannot have a corporate tax and then say spend another two percent. I am opposed to that."[58] He was articulating a view shared by most corporations in India who were firmly opposed to this new mandate. They too argued that a higher tax rate made more sense than the requirements of the 2013 Companies Act under Section 135. The Chairman of the Federation of Chambers of Commerce in India pleaded against mandatory CSR.[59] But they were overruled, and the law was adopted anyway. Given the resistance by organized business groups and by one of the chief advocates of neoliberal economic policies, some other explanation must be found for the passage of the law. The neoliberal story has much to recommend it as a description of the *effects* of Article 135 but is not supported as a catalyst for the law.

Foreign Aid Story

Damien Krichewsky offers two explanations for the rise of CSR in India.[60] First, he suggests a social systems approach to understand why CSR in general has become so prominent as a solution to the tensions of the past two decades. Second, he offers a narrower story of how German foreign aid helped to introduce and support passage of mandatory CSR in the form of Article 135. The first argument is that as India has seen greater functional differentiation between the economy, politics, social morality, and so on, greater tension between the economic logic of the profit-seeking behavior of firms and their negative externalities has grown. As businesses operate more and more on the basis of economic rationality, they are unable to "read" the social context in which they operate. This creates space for political entrepreneurs to mobilize against businesses that create wealth for the few at the expense of the many. Their externalities (pollution, wealth inequality, labor insecurity) left unaddressed will limit the prospects for profit making. That's where CSR comes in. It makes businesses responsive to these problems, thus conserving their ability to make profits for the long run. Damien Krichewsky argues

---

58 Indian Express 2011. "Montek Opposes CSR 'Tax' *Indian Express* Available at http://indianexpress.com/article/news-archive/web/montek-opposes-csr-tax-on-companies/ (accessed December 2023).

59 Kumar, Rajiv. 2011; updated 2018. "Don't Make CSR Mandatory." *The Hindu* https://www.thehindubusinessline.com/opinion/columns/rajiv-kumar/dont-make-csr-mandatory/article20311363.ece1 (accessed June 7, 2021).

60 Kirchewesky, Damien. 2019. *Corporate Social Responsibility and Economic Responsiveness in India*, by Damien Krichewsky. Cambridge: Cambridge University Press.

THE MATCHMAKER STATE   59

that CSR is an intermediate institution that seeks to make the economic logic of business responsive to social needs.

Importantly, his book also tells a story of how consideration of regulation of CSR by the government came into the picture. Companies of course have had CSR programs for decades before the passage of 135. In 2008, the German foreign aid program launched a multiyear program targeting the India Ministry for Corporate Affairs—"Indo-German Corporate Social Responsibility Initiative." This initiative claimed to be a response to the fragmented nature of CSR in India and a lack of Indian understanding of the role it could play in sustainable economic development. "At the policy level, to develop and broaden consensus about CSR in the Indian context, the project is helping to establish a multi-stakeholder dialogue process at the Indian Institute of Corporate Affairs (IICA), which is a think-tank of the Ministry of Corporate Affairs. This involves a wide array of public, non-governmental and private-sector actors, and is being backed up by various studies and surveys."[61] By bringing together various stakeholders, the Germans were seeding the idea of developing guidelines for CSR that could be adopted across industries. However, a rival group within the Ministry rejected the German process and proposals in favor of their own approach to CSR. This group eventually created the Guidelines for Public Enterprises which went into effect in 2009 and were adapted for the private sector in 2013. I return to this group in the fourth story below.

Krichewsky makes a plausible argument for using a social system theoretical framework, one that stresses the functional relationships between elements, to understand CSR in India. That said, I think there are other plausible approaches to understanding CSR in India. For instance, his case study of LaFarge India[62] itself shows that although its CSR program was developed to silence critics and smooth the path for the creation of a new concrete plant, it failed, and LaFarge's Indian subsidiary decided not to build the plant because of political and social opposition. The evolution of the guidelines also shows that, rather than developing from the bottom up as businesses' response to their inability to "see" social problems, the introduction of these guidelines came about as a result of the German foreign aid agency searching for developing country partners. In both cases, one could tell a story of international norm diffusion. That is, CSR in India has grown and become institutionalized at least in part because of globalization. Multinational

---

61 Deutsche Gesellschaft fur Internationale Zusammerabeit. 2008. *Indo-German CSR Initiative* https://www.giz.de/en/worldwide/16623.html (accessed June 7, 2021).

62 La Farge is originally a French construction company that specialized in cement production in India. It only operated in India for about a decade.

CORPORATE SOCIAL RESPONSIBILITY AND CIVIL SOCIETY

corporations have brought their norms of CSR to India, and policymakers have been influenced by their contacts with early movers on CSR in more developed states. That is the argument made by Ursula Muhle who argues that CSR can be understood as an emergent global norm in the 2000s.[63] The way that this norm has been adapted into Article 135 in India, however, needs another explanation.

Caste Story

Starting in December 2004, the UPA government began to explore the idea of introducing reservations or quotas in the private sector for historically marginalized groups; Dalits and Adivasis. The response from the corporate sector was decidedly resistant. The head of Bajaj Autos wrote that industry had already hired a significant number of people from these oppressed groups and said that reservations would force them to hire subpar talent and hurt their production processes. The head of the Chambers of Indian Industry claimed that reservations would hurt efficiency and competitiveness while introducing discrimination into a caste-blind sector.[64] The immediate resistance of the private sector put a pause on the initiative. However, the political parties continued to include it in their election platforms.

In 2006, Meira Kumar, then Minister for Social Justice and Empowerment, spearheaded a second round of discussions on this topic. She convened a group of Ministers to work with industry to find a way forward. A former president of CII stated, "CII's position is very clear. Reservation in any form is simply not acceptable for it is not the solution to the problem of uplifting the socially underprivileged. I agree that the underprivileged need to break their own form of glass ceilings by becoming officers and executives, but let me tell you that there has never been any social bias against them. Industry is willing to work with government to build capabilities and bridge gaps, but at no time can they ram anything down our throats."[65]

The corporate sector offered affirmative action and skills training rather than quotas. That is, they argued they would train marginalized people and then promote them voluntarily rather than being held accountable by the state

---

63 Muhle, Ursula. 2010. *The Politics of Corporate Social Responsibility: The Rise of a Global Norm*. Frankfurt: Campus Verlag GmBH.

64 Thimmaiah, G. 2005 "Implications of Reservations in Private Sector." *Economic and Political Weekly*. 40(8), 745–750.

65 Bamzai, Sandeep. 2006. "Quota: India Inc must think fast" *Hindustan Times* May 9 Available at https://www.hindustantimes.com/india/quota-india-inc-must-think-fast/story-8JP48Zw5NbAEsiZ4JKbtLO.html (accessed May 9, 2024).

THE MATCHMAKER STATE   61

for greater inclusivity. The industry offer was the brainchild of Ratan Tata who brought along another 21 heads of major industrial houses to this compromise. "We will conduct training in-house as well as in partnership with IITs and vendor development programmes. We will do this through credible CSOs and self-help groups. In these and other ways, we shall implement in letter and spirit a programme of affirmative action to empower those who are socially and economically backward."[66] This seemed to pacify the politicians for a while.[67] One CSO leader described the process by which this letter was drafted and how it planted the seeds for an expansion of CSR activities.

"And that time Ratan Tata wrote a letter to business captains telling "Let us oppose it." So that letter came to [my main donor who] showed me the letter and said "Will you help me draft a reply"?

So, I said "You know I beg to differ with Ratan. You won't win this battle opposing it. This is in line with the current political climate we have to play differently."

He said, "Tell me what you will do."

I said "First of all create a CSR council. You declare you will fund 2%" (At that time it was not law).

He said, "Dude 2% is too much *yaar* [buddy] let's do 1%."

I said, "Okay 1% and you say that out of this money you will set up 6 schools meant for schedule caste schedule tribes."

That's the day I realized the f-ing power of government to make this freaking private sector shiver and I realized that private sector is so obsessed with shareholder value that they're shit scared of government. If I tell you as Prime Minister that I am increasing your company sector tax by 15% they will be like prostrated lying [on the ground] and saying *kya karna hai? bolo sahab* [what should I do? tell me sir] and I can like demand anything [...]. [If] you are a politician so I would say okay I need to play both because my constituency is the poor or the disenfranchised."[68]

---

66 Devi, Laxmi. 2005. "Does India Inc need job reservation?" *Economic Times* June 2. Available at https://economictimes.indiatimes.com/does-india-inc-need-job-reservation/articleshow/1129488.cms?utm_source=contentofinterest&utm_medium=text&utm_campaign=cppst (accessed June 8, 2021).

67 CNN-IBN June 1, 2006. "No Way Out" Available at https://web.archive.org/web/20060614183346/http://www.ibnlive.com/news/no-way-out-private-sector-has-to-implement-quota/12030-3.html (accessed July 26, 2024).

68 Personal Interview. October 1, 2019. Mumbai, India.

62   CORPORATE SOCIAL RESPONSIBILITY AND CIVIL SOCIETY

In this account, the fear that these captains of industry had of being forced to institute reservations pushed them to make a series of creative counterproposals. Some of them promoted the idea of affirmative action rather than quotas as more suitable for competitive businesses. Others began to systematize their CSR, move it outside the whims of the Chairman of the corporation, and develop a strategic CSR vision. These steps laid the groundwork for when the Ministry of Corporate Affairs became interested in CSR. These big industrialists could work with them and try to manage the drafting of the CSR guidelines into a similarly voluntary option. In the end, they were not able to prevent the bureaucracy and the politicians from getting their way and having a mandatory CSR law enacted in the form of 135. But they did diffuse the reservation reforms.

The caste story is one of a back-and-forth between industry and democratic representatives in which CSR is seen as a less dangerous alternative to higher taxes or more regulation of their actual business processes. This story, that caste—that defining social ill of India—catalyzed the development of the modern CSR landscape, is in keeping with work that shows how caste, class, and corporate interests dynamically shape economic policies.[69] It also suggests that it is not only material interests at play, but we also must consider the role social identity plays in driving both politics and markets.

Bureaucracy Story

In this fourth version of events, a lone enlightened bureaucrat championed the adoption of CSR guidelines for public sector enterprises and then steered parliament into adopting them for the private sector as well.[70] In 2019, I interviewed Bhaskar Chatterjee about being referred to as the "father of Indian CSR," which is usually how he is introduced at CSR summits and events. In 2009, he became the Principal Secretary for Public Enterprises and found a file with a few notes about CSR on his desk. This combined with what he was learning from his daughter who was working in a CSR partnership between her CSO and a British company piqued his interest. As he began asking the Directors of the Public Enterprises about their CSR and their overall impact on Indian society, he found that, "all the CSR was ad-hoc. There was no real public impact of it. A lot of it was directed at their own

---

69 Murali, Kanta. 2017. *Caste, Class and Capital: The Social and Political Origins of Economic Policy in India.* Cambridge, UK: Cambridge University Press.

70 This account was confirmed by another senior bureaucrat at the Indian Institute of Corporate Affairs in a personal interview with the author (New Delhi 2019).

THE MATCHMAKER STATE 63

employees."[71] From this point onwards, he worked on CSR for the next decade until it was fully institutionalized. In his account, the driving force for Article 135 was technocratic. It was about increasing governmentality and regulation over corporate enterprises that were failing to serve the public good.

In describing the process by which Article 135 was adopted, Chatterjee reminisced about his advice to Minister for Corporate Affair V. Moily and Junior Minister Sachin Pilot as follows:

"The way in which we presented CSR made it impossible to oppose. I told Mr Moily that we had to link it to the development agenda of the nation. Once we did that it became unassailable. We asked, "should development and uplift of the poor be the responsibility only of the government? We all know the deficiencies of the government. There are issues of leakages, bureaucratic formalities, the rigidity and all the others we all know. Therefore, the private sector can also step forward and be a partner in development. The private sector brings innovation, agility, dynamism, capacity to monitor, and efficiency." We showed that we were giving the corporates a final chance to be involved in nation building. You know in December 2013 when Pilot had to spend 10 hours in parliament defending the Companies Act, he spent six hours on the CSR provisions. Everyone in parliament supported it. They had to. See we said "out of the 1000k companies registered in India this act only affects about 14–15000. Those are the fat cats. Where are they getting their profits?" So, once we were talking about fat cats and development needs, everyone was on board."[72]

Essentially, the bureaucracy was able to frame the CSR provisions in a way that made it impossible for politicians to speak out against them.[73] The political platform of "Inclusive Growth" used in the 2009 elections forced them to support Article 135 once it was framed as a way to make the big winners of liberalization to do their fair share for national development. The bureaucracy in India has long been seen as an important site of policymaking, partially responsive to political pressures but also somewhat autonomous.[74] This is a case in which the state is not seeking to withdraw from the public provision

---

71 Chatterjee, Bhaskar. 2019. Personal Interview New Delhi (August 21).

72 Chatterjee, Bhaskar. 2019. Personal Interview New Delhi (August 21).

73 Benford, R. D. and David Snow. 2000. "Framing Processes and Social Movements: An Overview and Assessment." *Annual Review of Sociology.* 26(1), 611–639.

74 Weiner, Myron. 1991. *The Child and the State in India.* Princeton. NJ: Princeton University Press; Sinha, Aseema. 2005. *The Regional Roots of Developmental Politics in India: A Divided Leviathan.* Bloomington, IN: Indiana University Press; Bhavnani, Rikhil and Alexander Lee. 2018. "Local Embeddedness and Bureaucratic Performance: Evidence from India." *Journal of Politics.* 80(1), 71–87.

64   CORPORATE SOCIAL RESPONSIBILITY AND CIVIL SOCIETY

of development goods. Rather it is a case where the state is acting to enforce its role as matchmaker between the private and non-profit sectors. It is asserting jurisdiction over both.

This story of the adoption of CSR provisions is one in which a passion project for a senior bureaucrat was advanced using the political framing of inclusive growth to build political support. The objections of the public sector enterprises were dismissed, then those of the private sector could not be catered to, and thus a consensus on Article 135 emerged. In this version of events, the driving force for CSR rules is the bureaucracy which sought to expand its role in governing corporate activities. Therefore, Article 135 should be seen as an expansion of the state's governing power rather than an attempt to hide its recusal from the provision of social services.

Conclusion

The constitution of the post-colonial state in India committed the government to extensive involvement in economic development as part of its task of nation-building. The work of delivering equality and justice in terms of political, civil, and economic rights was seen as the work of the state. Disillusionment with this developmental nation-building project reached significant levels in the 1970s. This critical juncture reshaped relations between civil society organizations and the state from being closely collaborative to a more contentious watchdog model. The end of the Cold War brought with it international support for civil society and a major push to diminish the role of the state in the market and in public goods provision. These dual dynamics reshaped civil society into a service delivery agency in partnership and/or in competition with the state. Meanwhile, economic liberalization led to the privatization of some state assets, the deregulation of the market, and a growth in crony capitalism as some large corporations were able to take advantage of the new dispensation.

Today civil society is simultaneously under attack by the state and also being coopted by it in a variety of developmental projects. Meanwhile, civil society activists seek to harness the power of the state to scale up their programs and to resist corporate visions of economic growth at the expense of people and the natural environment. These complicated dynamics of collaboration, cooption, and contestation make up the state-civil society relationship today. While many see the BJP as the driving force behind these dynamics, in this chapter I showed that many of them were set in motion by the previous Congress-led government. The history is not just about one political party. Rather, we have to pay attention to the variety of types of

CSOs as well as the multiple agendas contained within each government to make sense of the state and civil society relationship.

This history and these relationships are key to making sense of how Article 135 was created and how it is being used today. In this chapter, I described four stories of its origins and in the next few chapters, I will describe its impacts. Article 135, requiring companies to spend 2% of their annual profits on social causes, largely through partnerships with CSOs, passed in 2013 after about five years of discussion about CSR among Indian politicians, bureaucrats, corporations, and foreign aid advisors. The civil society sector was not a significant player in the creation of this vast new channel of resources even though it is hugely impacted by it.

The passage of Article 135 despite corporate resistance is explained in four ways. In the neoliberalism story, the state uses CSR to cover up its own failure to provide public goods and as a way to prettify corporate profits. In the foreign aid story, 135 is a result of norm diffusion from Germany to India and reflects the greater absorption of India into the global political economy. The third story suggests that corporate India was willing to impose costly CSR rules on itself as a way to avoid even costlier regulations requiring caste-based reservations in the private sector. Finally, the bureaucracy narrative suggests that the state actually is reasserting its power over business (public and private) by pushing corporations to consider the public interest as their profits keep growing.

The neoliberalism story is one that many critics tell, but I show that while it may explain the work that 135 is doing now, there isn't much evidence to support it as an origin story. While the German aid program did lead to some initial discussions about CSR in the Ministry of Corporate Affairs it wasn't until the bureaucracy and politicians became interested that the conversation moved into action. The framing of the rules as mandatory was not supported by the Germans and is clearly an Indian innovation. The resistance to 135 perhaps was not as intense as public statements would suggest because many of the largest corporations had already adopted similar policies as a way to head off caste-based quotas. This story suggests that caste supremacy and identity drove the adoption of 135 rather than economic interests. Given what we know about how white supremacy and savarna supremacy shape-shift and find innovative ways to maintain the status quo even as demands for equality and justice arise, I think this narrative should be taken quite seriously and explored further. Finally, at the micro-level, the role played by a motivated bureaucrat- Chatterjee- is a clear example of how the Indian state remains committed to its core ideals even as parts of it embrace neoliberal ideology. 135 is a way for the government to nudge the corporate sector to act in the interests of nation building through economic development and inclusion at the direction of the state.

66   CORPORATE SOCIAL RESPONSIBILITY AND CIVIL SOCIETY

Each of these stories has elements of truth to them. CSR is a brilliant marketing tool for corporations that allows them to deflect attention from their core business processes and allows them to posture as altruistic philanthropists. Global norms of doing business include norms of appearing to "do good" and are useful for Indian companies as they become more internationally competitive and have multinational operations. CSR is a less painful way to perform social inclusion than to actually restructure economic power and opportunity away from savarna formations towards historically oppressed groups. The mandatory aspects of 135 (and later reforms) are a way for the state to reclaim some of its power over corporations to fold them into the larger nation-building project. Where partisans of hegemony theory may be satisfied with the first story, most sociologists, historians, and political scientists should accept the complexity of all four stories revealing varying, but true, aspects of reality.

The matchmaker state, brokering partnerships between CSOs and corporate houses is not simply a tool of hegemonic capital. It is also not a simple recipient of diplomatic advice and capacity building. It is a site for contestation over identity politics, resources, and nation building. It is a site for contestation and also a player or an agent within these battles. While it often serves the interests of the powerful, its power can also be deployed in service of humbling the wealthy. The matchmaker state created Article 135 with the expectation that it would lead to new efficiencies and innovation in the social sector. The next chapters examine to what extent these expectations are being realized.

Chapter 3

INCLUSIVE AND SUSTAINABLE DEVELOPMENT

Sustainable development, "meets the needs of the present without compromising the ability of future generations to meet their own needs."[1] This widely accepted definition was offered by the Brundtland Commission to argue for multilateral approaches to rethinking growth and environmental linkages. The definition is one that recognizes the importance of time in thinking about sustainability, makes visible the obligations current generations have to our descendants, and highlights the need for better distribution of resources to meet current needs. Sustainability speaks to the ability of a thing or a process to last over time. It indicates that the time periods of relevance are not simply the next quarter or next five years, but rather multiple generations.[2] The human tendency to heavily discount the future needs to be countered by this commitment to future generations for whom we have caretaking obligations.

The acknowledgment of current needs in the definition speaks to the highly uneven distribution of resources and consumption in the present. Brundtland wrote that the environment and development were inseparable as, "the 'environment' is where we all live; and 'development' is what we all do in attempting to improve our lot within that abode [...] Many of the development paths of the industrialised nations are clearly unsustainable [...] These links between poverty, inequality, and environmental degradation formed a major theme in our analysis and recommendations. What is needed now is a new era of economic growth— growth that is forceful and at the same time socially and environmentally

---

1 Brundtland Commission. 1987. "Our Common Future" Available at https:// sustainabledevelopment.un.org/content/documents/5987our-common-future.pdf (accessed May 12, 2022).

2 The principle of seven generations is based on a Haudenosaunee ideal of decisions taken today being beneficial for the next seven generations. See https://www. haudenosauneeconfederacy.com/values/ (accessed May 12, 2022).

68   CORPORATE SOCIAL RESPONSIBILITY AND CIVIL SOCIETY

sustainable." The high consumption of wealthy countries is unsustainable. And the denial of resources to the poor is unsustainable.

Thinking about time and beyond the lens of consumption, Sudhir Anand and Amartya Sen argue that the central idea of sustainability is intergenerational equity. They point out that the lives of future generations should be of equal concern to us as the lives of those today. Anand and Sen argue that, if poverty is our target, wealth maximization should not be our only tool. "The most basic problem with the opulence view is its comprehensive failure to take note of the need for impartial concern in looking at the real opportunities individuals have. The exclusive concentration only on incomes [...] ignores the plurality of influences that differentiate the real opportunities of people."[3] That is, income fails to consider the natural environment or cultural context in which people live their lives. Inclusive development could go some way toward directing our attention to those aspects but is all too often simply treated as referring to the need to include all people in income maximization. Amartya Sen makes a broader suggestion—that the focus on material needs is too narrow a conception of human needs. Because we are also value-driven creatures, we may wish to sustain the environment for reasons beyond our inter-generational ability to make use of it. He suggests thinking about sustainable freedom—that we must preserve and when possible, expand freedom today without compromising the ability of future generations to enjoy similarly broad freedom.[4]

In 2015, the UN adopted the Sustainable Development Goals to replace the Millennium Development Goals to focus the world's attention and accountability on development that was not only about growth but also sustainability. Where the MDGs created targets for reductions in maternal mortality and access to education in the Global South, the SDGs also have targets for Global North countries to meet regarding their consumption and production processes.[5] There are a number of critics of the SDGs who see them as so vague that they fail to hold states accountable for their failure to actually meet them.[6] Still, there is widespread

---

3 Anand, Sudhir and Amartya Sen. 2000. "Human Development and Economic Sustainability." *World Development*. 28(12), 2029–2049.

4 Sen, Amartya. 2009. *The Idea of Justice*. Allen Lane: London, UK. (pp 248–252).

5 Carant, Jane B. 2017 "Unheard Voices: A Critical Discourse Analysis of the Millennium Development Goals' Evolution into the Sustainable Development Goals." *Third World Quarterly*. 38(1), 16–41, doi: 10.1080/01436597.2016.1166944

6 Alston, Phillip. 2020. "The Parlous State of Poverty Eradication" Report of the UN Special Rapporteur on extreme poverty and human rights" https://digitallibrary.un.org/record/3904295?ln=en&v=pdf (accessed May 10, 2024) and Horton, Richard. 2014. "Offline: Why the Sustainable Development Goals will fail." *Lancet*. 383, 9936. Pg 2196, June 28.

INCLUSIVE AND SUSTAINABLE DEVELOPMENT 69

support for the actual text and goals included in the SDGs by states and development agencies. These goals include ending extreme poverty, hunger; achieving good health, education, sanitation, decent work conditions, peace, justice and industrial innovation; producing clean energy sustainable urban planning, responsible consumption, climate action, preserving marine and land ecosystems; all while reducing inequalities and building partnerships to tackle these global agendas.[7] The SDGs are ambitious and capacious goals and they have been agreed upon by the UN's member nations giving them widespread reach and legitimacy.

In the business sector, sustainability is broadly thought of as a firm or process that can reproduce itself without requiring fresh infusions of investment. There have been over 500 attempts to create measurement tools to operationalize sustainable business. The ambiguity of the term leads to this profusion of measures and an accompanying confusion about what exactly sustainable business does. The identification of goals in which the business has a neutral or positive impact on the environment and society leads to some clarity but is not broadly generalizable.[8] The ideal of sustainability is a growth process that considers the economy, the environment, and society. The third pillar is one that received the least attention until quite recently.[9] This third pillar is where the importance of "inclusivity" comes into focus. It is also the most controversial, especially in the USA where prominent critics like Presidential candidate Vivek Ramaswamy have made a political career out of condemning companies that think beyond shareholder profit.[10]

Due to the primacy of growth and environmental sustainability, the work of social movements led to the addition of inclusivity as a critical aspect of sustainable development.[11] Inclusive of what? Inclusivity refers to the need

---

7 United Nations. 2015. Sustainable Development Goals Available at https://sdgs.un.org/2030agenda Accessed May 16, 2022.

8 Parris, Thomas M. and Robert W. Kates. 2003. "Characterizing and Measuring Sustainable Development." *Annual Review of Environment and Resources.* 28(1), 559–586. Porter, M. E. and M. R. Kramer .2011. Creating Shared Value. *Harvard Business Review.* 89(1/2), 62–77.

9 Strange, T. and A. Bayley. 2008. *Sustainable Development: Linking Economy, Society, Environment.* Paris: OECD Insights, OECD Publishing, https://doi.org/10.1787/9789264055742-en.

10 Ramaswamy, Vivek. 2021. *Woke Inc: Inside Corporate America's Social Justice Scam.* New York, NY: Hatchett Books.

11 Pouw, Nicky and Joyeeta Gupta. 2017. "Inclusive development: a multi-disciplinary approach." *Current Opinion in Environmental Sustainability.* 24, 104–108. https://doi.org/10.1016/j.cosust.2016.11.013; Gupta, Joyeta and Courtney Vegelin. 2016.

70   CORPORATE SOCIAL RESPONSIBILITY AND CIVIL SOCIETY

to center the most marginalized people as development goals are created and pursued. That is, inclusivity emphasizes the social dimension of sustainability specifically by drawing attention to marginalized individuals and communities. This is because these people are the ones who are the first to suffer the consequences of environmental degradation and are the least able to cushion themselves from the negative effects of the growth process.[12] Beyond pointing to the most vulnerable communities, the concept of inclusive development also demands a rethinking of the goals of development beyond simply reducing negative aspects of growth to asking if growth itself is the appropriate goal of economic activity.[13] While this transformative question is rarely centered, the language of inclusivity can nudge decision-makers to at least pose systemic and normative questions as they chart development agendas.

Poverty

What is poverty? Poverty is a lack of resources *and* a denial of dignity. The combination of material deprivation and social exclusion captures both the absolute and relative definitions of poverty. Absolute poverty is defined by an income below $2.15 by the United Nations, World Bank, and other official bodies. Relative poverty speaks to the experience of deprivation more closely linked with context.[14] A person in Finland is relatively poor because they have inadequate heat, transport, or a smartphone even if they would actually be considered middle class in Bangladesh because they do have shelter, adequate calorie intake, and access to a health clinic. However, the inability of the Finn to participate in social life and the labor market marks them as poor within their own society.

The fact that poverty is a social condition and not just a material condition is at the heart of the inclusion approach to tackling development.

Sustainable Development Goals and Inclusive Development. *International Environmental Agreements.* 16, 433–448. https://doi.org/10.1007/s10784-016-9323-z.

12 Mohai, Paul, David Pellow, and J. Timmons Robersts. 2009. "Environmental Justice" *Annual Review of Environment and Resources.* 35, 405–430; Scholsberg, David. 2013. "Theorising Environmental Justice." *Environmental Politics.* 22(1), 37–55.

13 Deeming, C and P. Smyth (Eds). 2018. *Reframing Global Social Policy: Social Investment for Sustainable and Inclusive Growth.* Bristol, UK: Policy Press.

14 Dhongde, S. 2010. "Measuring Global Poverty." *Oxford Encyclopaedia of International Studies.* Oxford, UK: Oxford University Press; Escobar, A. 1995. *Encountering Development: The Making and Unmaking of the Third World.* Princeton, NJ: Princeton University Press; Hulme, D, and A. Shepherd, (Eds.). 2003. *Conceptualising Poverty.* London, UK: Routledge.

INCLUSIVE AND SUSTAINABLE DEVELOPMENT 71

The social and psychological dimensions of deprivation, exploitation, and exclusion are what define the experience of poverty. Therefore, development cannot be only about ensuring a minimum basket of goods. Rather, it must be about asking what is needed to live a decent life. The capabilities approach created by Amartya Sen, Martha Nussbaum, and others is one that asks us to move from asking about the distribution of resources to thinking about the distribution of capabilities to lead a self-defined good life.[15] This is in contrast to more utilitarian views that often drive policymaking through a logic of "the greatest good for the greatest number" assuming that preferences are similar across people and time. The capabilities approach focuses on what people want and what resources and relationships they need to achieve those desires. A utilitarian approach, like Peter Singer's, assumes we know what people want and tries to give as many individuals the resources policymakers think are most important.[16] Increasingly the approach that we need to think about poverty as a social problem even more than an economic one is gaining acceptance. In his scathing critique of foreign aid, economist Angus Deacon writes, "If poverty is not the result of lack of resources or opportunities, but of poor institutions, poor government, and toxic politics, giving money to poor countries—particularly giving money to the *governments* of poor countries— is likely to perpetuate and prolong poverty, not eliminate it."[17] Once we see that poverty is an economic, social, and political phenomena, we must expand our response to it beyond the reformist approaches that dominate most development interventions.

What does inclusivity mean in the Indian context? Another way to think about this, is what are the social bases of exclusion? There are a number of axes along which exclusion is broadly universal—gender, sexuality, class, and disability. These are aspects of identity that are tied to access to resources, roles within the production process, bases for social exclusion, and hierarchy in most societies. In addition to these, in India, we should also consider the role of region, religion, and caste as consequential dimensions of identity and inequality. A person's gender identity, sexuality, class location, ability, state, religious community, and caste location all

---

15 Nussbaum, M.C. and A. Sen. 1993. *The Quality of Life*. Oxford: Clarendon Press Oxford; Sen, A. 1999. *Development as Freedom*. Anchor Books; Nussbaum, M. C. 2000. *Women and Human Development: The Capabilities Approach*. Cambridge University Press.

16 Singer, Peter. 2009. *The Life You Can Save*. New York, NY: Random House.

17 Deaton, Angus. 2013. *The Great Escape: Health, Wealth, and the Origins of Inequality*. Princeton, NJ: Princeton University Press.

CORPORATE SOCIAL RESPONSIBILITY AND CIVIL SOCIETY

predict their degree of inclusion or exclusion in Indian political, economic, and social life. In the next section, I discuss some of these and show how access to resources and social standing are linked in the Indian context, before turning to the historical processes that support and sustain these exclusions.

Inclusion and Exclusion in India

Class

Poverty is probably the least controversial way to measure exclusion and deprivation. India has the largest number of poor people of any country in the world, along with the biggest overall population as of 2023. Globally, 685 million people live in extreme poverty, which is defined as living on less than $2:15 per day by the International Poverty Line measure.[18] Of this deprived population, India is home to almost 143 million extremely poor citizens based on the IPL.[19] Another measure, the Multidimensional Poverty Index (MPI), takes into account more factors than the international poverty line measure which only captures income. The MPI goes beyond income, to the daily deprivations that people living in poverty experience—deprivations of health, education, and quality of life. The MPI gets more specific by creating a deprivation score for an impoverished person through assessing ten indicators of deprivation ranging from nutrition to school attendance to access to housing. This measure suggests that actually 1.2 billion from 111 countries making up 19.1 percent of the world population live in acute multidimensional poverty. Half of the most deprived people (593 million) are children. In India, the poor are most likely to lack adequate nutrition, cooking fuel, sanitation, and safe housing and number 230 million.[20] As one CSO

---

18 World Bank. 2022. "Measuring Poverty." Available at https://www.worldbank.org/en/topic/measuringpoverty (accessed September 2023).

19 World Bank. 2023. "Data Bank." Available at https://data.worldbank.org/indicator/SI.POV.DDAY?end=2021&locations=IN&start=1977&view=chart (accessed September 2023).

20 UNDP and OPHI. 2022. Global Multidimensional Poverty Index 2022: Unpacking Deprivation Bundles to Reduce Multidimensional Poverty. United Nations Development Programme (UNDP), and Oxford Poverty and Human Development Initiative (OPHI), University of Oxford. Available at https://hdr.undp.org/content/2022-global-multidimensional-poverty-index-mpi#/indicies/MPI (accessed May 13, 2024).

INCLUSIVE AND SUSTAINABLE DEVELOPMENT

leader said, "Poverty issues are not linear—they are all linked. That's why our work has to be cluster based and holistic."[21]

The reduction in poverty in India has been remarkable—about 415 million people escaped poverty since 2015. There are likely some reversals caused by the COVID pandemic that are not yet reflected in the data but the fact remains that for the poorest Indians, the past decade has offered new hope. Even more heartening is the fact that the fastest reductions in poverty took place in India's poorest states. "There have been visible investments in boosting access to sanitation, cooking fuel and electricity—indicators that have seen large improvements. A policy emphasis on universal coverage—for example, in education, nutrition, water, sanitation, employment and housing—likely contributed to these results."[22] As more Indians can access the basic goods and services for a dignified life the fact remains that resources and opportunities remain unevenly accessible.

Looking at inequality, the average annual income of an Indian adult is INR204,200 ($2544). But where the bottom 50% earns INR53,610 ($644), the top 10% earns more than 20 times that amount. "While the top 10% and top 1% hold respectively 57% and 22% of total national income, the bottom 50% share has gone down to 13%. India stands out as a poor and very unequal country, with an affluent elite."[23] What accounts for this inequality? According to Tista Kundu, "Our research indicated that at least 30% of earning inequality is still determined by caste, gender and family backgrounds." This is compared with below 10% in the most egalitarian societies. Her team calculates that of the 30%, 7% of inequality of opportunity is driven by caste discrimination while gender and family make up the remainder.[24] That is, the distribution of income and opportunities to earn income often depend on structural, social inequalities. As we learn that, "[t]he hydraulic approach to aid is wrong, and fixing poverty is nothing like fixing a broken car or pulling

---

21 Pallasanna, Krishnan. 2019. "Cluster based CSR collaboration" CSR Box Summit New Delhi.

22 UNDP and OPHI. 2022. Global Multidimensional Poverty Index 2022: Unpacking Deprivation Bundles to Reduce Multidimensional Poverty. United Nations Development Programme (UNDP), and Oxford Poverty and Human Development Initiative (OPHI), University of Oxford. Page 22. Available at https://hdr.undp.org/content/2022-global-multidimensional-poverty-index-mpi#/indicies/MPI (accessed May 13, 2024).

23 Chancel, L., T. Piketty, E. Saez, G. Zucman et al. World Inequality Report 2022, World Inequality Lab Available at https://wir2022.wid.world/www-site/uploads/2022/03/0098-21_WIL_RIM_RAPPORT_A4.pdf (accessed July 2023).

24 Kundu, Tista. 2022. "The Multiple Faces of Inequality in India" The Conversation. Available at https://theconversation.com/the-multiple-faces-of-inequality-in-india-182074 Accessed August 2023.

CORPORATE SOCIAL RESPONSIBILITY AND CIVIL SOCIETY

a drowning child out of a shallow pool [...] The technical, anti-political view of development assistance" looks increasingly ineffective.[25]

Gender

One of the most significant forms of *social* discrimination can be seen in the differences in outcomes and opportunities based on gender. The Gender Development Index compares female to male health (life expectancy at birth), education (expected years of schooling for children and mean years of schooling for adults aged 25 years and older), and income (estimated GNI per capita). Based on these comparisons, for 2021 India has a GDI value of 0.849, which ranks it 127th out of 146 countries. Essentially the female human development index value for India is 0.567 in contrast with 0.668 for males. While women are expected to live longer than men (68.9:65.8), their education access is lower (6.3 years for women over 25 compared to 7.2 years for adult men), and most disparate of all is the income differential ($2,277:$10,633) which shows that men have around 4.5 times the income of women.[26] The skewed sex ratios found in India have been estimated to mean that about 400,000 girls are "missing" at birth. That is, these female fetuses were aborted due to their sex. In addition, another 240,000 girls die due to postnatal discrimination before their fifth birthday.[27] The gender imbalance seems to be narrowing over the past decade, especially among the wealthier and higher caste communities that previously had the greatest imbalance.[28] Third-gender (trans) individuals surveyed in the 2011 census numbered almost half a million and were found to have a literacy rate of 56.07% as compared with men just over 80% and women at 65.46%.[29]

Looking at the Gender Inequality Index, India has a GII value of 0.490, ranking it 122 out of 170 countries in 2021. This index combines data on reproductive health, political representation, and formal labor market

---

25 Deaton, Angus. 2013. *The Great Escape: Health, Wealth, and the Origins of Inequality.* Princeton, NJ: Princeton University Press.

26 UNDP. 2022. Human Development Reports: India. Available at https://hdr.undp.org/data-center/specific-country-data#/countries/IND (accessed January 2023).

27 UNFPA. 2021. "Sex ratio at birth in India: Recent trends and patterns." Available at https://india.unfpa.org/en/news/sex-ratio-birth-india-recent-trends-and-patterns (accessed September 2023).

28 Pew Research Center. 2022. "India's Sex Ratio at Birth Begins to Normalize." Available at https://www.pewresearch.org/religion/2022/08/23/indias-sex-ratio-at-birth-begins-to-normalize/ (accessed September 2023).

29 Census of India 2011. https://www.census2011.co.in/transgender.php and https://www.census2011.co.in/literacy.php (accessed September 2022).

INCLUSIVE AND SUSTAINABLE DEVELOPMENT

participation. India historically had a particularly high rate of maternal mortality which has only recently declined to below the global average as more births have taken place under medical care.[30] Currently, less than 14% of seats in parliament are held by women, despite a long history of prominent women leaders.[31] The Indian parliament just passed a Women's Reservation Bill in Fall 2023 that will require a third of seats in national and state assemblies to be held by women but the legislation must be ratified by at least half the states to go into effect.[32] Presumably, this will shift India's ranking if the Bill is adopted before the 2024 parliamentary election. There is also a marked gap in formal labor force participation with less than a fifth of women working outside the home as compared with 70% of men.[33] Looking at beliefs about gender reveals that Indians hold discriminatory views against women.[34] Almost half of men and women believe intimate partner violence against women is justified in some cases and nearly a third of women report being subjected to violence in the home.[35] Altogether a picture of systematic gender inequality and discrimination emerges from these statistics.

The causes of social exclusion on the basis of gender are complicated to identify and even more so to undo. The patriarchal control over women's reproductive abilities is crucial to ensuring endogamous marriages are the norm in Indian society. As long as endogamous marriages are the norm, caste boundaries can be maintained. In fact, B. R. Ambedkar pointed out in 1935 that, "The real remedy for breaking Caste is intermarriage. Nothing

---

30 GOI. 2022. "Significant decline in maternal mortality in India" Ministry of Women and Child Development Available at https://pib.gov.in/FeaturesDeatils. aspx?NoteId=151238&ModuleId%20=%202 (accessed September 2023).

31 Deo, Nandini. 2012. "Dynastic Democracies" Gateway House Available at https://www.gatewayhouse.in/dynastic-democracies/ (accessed July 2016).

32 Phukan, Sandeep. 2023. "Lok Sabha passes historic women's reservation Bill" *The Hindu* September 20. Available at https://www.thehindu.com/news/national/lok-sabha-passes-womens-reservation-bill/article67327458.ece (accessed September 2023).

33 UNDP. 2022. Human Development Reports: India Available at https://hdr.undp.org/data-center/specific-country-data#/countries/IND (accessed April 2023).

34 UNDP. 2023. Gender Social Norms Index Report Available at https://hdr.undp.org/content/2023-gender-social-norms-index-gsni#/indicies/GSNI (accessed September 2023).

35 Parihar, Pragati. 2023. "Around 30% of Married Indian Women Have Experienced Gender Based Violence: Study" *Feminism in India* Available at https://feminisminindia. com/2023/05/30/30-married-indian-women-experienced-gender-based-violence/ (accessed September 2023).

76 CORPORATE SOCIAL RESPONSIBILITY AND CIVIL SOCIETY

else will serve as the solvent of Caste,"[36] and he identified the control of women's bodies through endogamy as the root cause of caste discrimination as early as 1917 in his work *Castes in India*.[37] The control over women's ability to engage in sex and marriage is needed to maintain caste boundaries. I will discuss caste as a basis for social exclusion below, but for now, it is important to flag the way in which attempts to equalize gender relations in India are also the most effective way to undermine caste exclusions. Caste cannot exist without community control over young people's love (sex) lives.

Nivedita Menon explains the foundational role of the family in creating a variety of social exclusions:

> There is a certain social order based on caste hierarchy, community identities, extreme class inequality, compulsory institution of heterosexual marriage, and the family that emerges or is sanctified by the heterosexual patriarchal marriage. It is this family that will give you your caste identity, your religious community identity; it will tell you where you are in the social system, and give you your privileges, and discrimination. Family is at the base of every single inequality in the modern society in which we live.[38]

It is this connection between gender roles within the family and most other forms of exclusion that best shows how intersectionality shows up in India. Each form of social exclusion is connected with others and those who experience deprivation do so from a social location defined by multiple identities. Inclusion therefore requires more than an additive approach in which a development project also includes disabled or queer individuals. Inclusion requires transformation of multiple spheres of identity and action simultaneously. It also means that inclusion is a highly explosive demand—it requires a radical change in society from the most intimate sphere of the family to the wider realms of employment and electoral participation.

---

36 Ambedkar, B. R. 1935. *The Annihilation of Caste* Available at https://ccnmtl.columbia. edu/projects/mmt/ambedkar/web/readings/aoc_print_2004.pdf (Pg 31).

37 Ambedkar, B. R. 1917. *Castes in India: Their Mechanism, Genesis and Development* Available at https://en.wikipedia.org/wiki/Castes_in_India:_Their_Mechanism,_Genesis_ and_Development.

38 Menon, Nivedita. 2022. "Gender attitudes in India: What's changed and what hasn't" *India Development Review* Podcast Available at https://idronline.org/podcasts/on-the-contrary-podcast-social-impact/gender-equality-where-are-we-today/ (accessed July 2023).

Caste

Exclusion in India has long been identified with caste discrimination. In recent decades, activists have come to frame this discrimination as caste apartheid, identifying the struggle with broader fights for racial equality and human rights.[39] Caste is a way of stratifying and exploiting labor legitimized by Hindu scriptures. It is inherited at birth and cannot be escaped in one lifetime. Through endogamous marriage within caste groups, caste is maintained. Besides shaping marriage and family life, caste historically determined access to education, food norms, professional pathways, land ownership, customary forced labor, and should be understood as ubiquitous and pervasive. Hindus are not the only ones to observe caste, in fact all religious groups in India have adopted caste identities and norms to some extent. Since 1931, the Indian census has avoided collecting data on most caste groups, except for the most disadvantaged scheduled castes (SCs) and scheduled tribes (STs).[40] The majority of Indians belong to these, or other backward castes (OBCs) and only about a quarter either have no caste identity or belong to a privileged caste (general category). According to data from the 2021 National Family Health Survey, across India, 22% are in the general category, 5% have no caste, 22% are SC, 10% are ST, and 42% are OBCs. The exact proportions vary by religion but large majorities of Sikh, Muslim, and Christian Indians also practice caste discrimination.[41] Genetic evidence shows that less than 5% of Indians marry outside their caste group, and that figure has been quite stable over centuries.[42] But how does caste shape lives?

Starting with wealth, as Zacharias and Vakulabharanam have noted, "inequality between castes (between-group inequality) accounts for as much as 8% to 13% of overall wealth inequality. The major determinant of between-group inequality is the large gap between SC/ST groups (especially rural)

---

39 Bob, C. 2007. "Dalit Rights are Human Rights": Caste Discrimination, International Activism, and the Construction of a New Human Rights Issue. *Human Rights Quarterly.* 29(1), 167–193; Kurien, Prema A. "The Racial Paradigm and Dalit Anti-Caste Activism in the United States," *Social Problems.* 70(3), August 2023, 717–734; Chitnis, Rucha. 2015. "Meet the Women Trying to Take Down 'Caste Apartheid'" *Yes* October 23. Available at https://www.yesmagazine.org/social-justice/2015/10/23/meet-the-women-trying-to-take-down-indias-caste-apartheid-and-finding-hope-in-black-lives-matter (accessed May 2022).

40 Saurav, Sandeep. 2022. "Why a caste census is the need of the hour" *The Wire* Available at https://thewire.in/caste/why-a-caste-census-is-the-need-of-the-hour (accessed September 2023).

41 NFHS 2019–2021. Available at https://rchiips.org/nfhs/ (accessed August 2023).

42 Munshi, K. 2019. "Caste and the Indian Economy." *Journal of Economic Literature.* 57(4), 781–834.

and the forward castes (especially urban) in average wealth."[43] However, the authors of this paper note, the rural/urban divisions within caste groups are actually even larger in accounting for wealth inequality. The fact is that there is of course considerable within-caste variation in consumption, wealth, and financial inclusion. Despite this, because land holding in rural areas is tied to access to banking and education, the oppressed castes have much higher rates of poverty than dominant castes.[44] In terms of occupational mobility, while some small-scale studies suggested that oppressed castes may be best able to take advantage of new opportunities offered by economic globalization,[45] broader studies reveal little support for the assumption that modernization, and specifically, urbanization would weaken the relationship between caste and occupational destination.[46] One review concluded, "Caste has transformed, with members of some castes acquiring economic and social advantages to maintain their edge in the labor market while denying members of other castes similar opportunities."[47]

Turning to education, Haldar introduces a large new dataset on college graduates in India (1856–2017), to show that educational mobility during this period was extremely low at the level of caste groups. Her dissertation shows that caste is a hindrance to the accumulation of human capital and social mobility in the long run.[48] Caste and gender interact in surprising ways. One innovative study showed that affirmative action policies targeted at SCs increased educational attainment among SC males but not females from 1977 to 1999.[49] Another study showed that because discrimination stopped SC males from converting formal schooling into better jobs and status,

---

43 Zacharias, A and Vamsi Vakulabharanam, "Caste Stratification and Wealth Inequality in India." *World Development.* 39(10), 2011, 1820–1833.

44 Tiwari, C., S. Goli, M. S. Siddiqui, and P. Salve. 2022. Poverty, Wealth Inequality, and Financial Inclusion among Castes in Hindu and Muslim Communities in Uttar Pradesh, India, *Journal of International Development.*

45 Luke, Nancy and Kaivan Munshi. 2011. "Women as Agents of Change: Female Income and Mobility in India." *Journal of Development Economics.* 94(1), 1–17.

46 Vaid, D., and A. F. Heath. 2010. Unequal Opportunities: Class, Caste and Social Mobility. In Diversity and Change in Modern India: Economic, Social and Political Approaches, ed. AF Heath, R Jeffery. Proc. Br. Acad. 159, pp. 129–164. Oxford, UK: Oxford University Press.

47 Vaid, Divya. 2014. "Caste in Contemporary India: Flexibility and Persistence." *Annual Review of Sociology.* 40(1), 391–410.

48 Haldar, Tamoghana. 2021. "Social Mobility and Segregation in a Caste-based Society: Bengal, 1850–2020" Dissertation UC Davis.

49 Cassan, Guilhem. 2019. "Affirmative Action, Education and Gender: Evidence from India." *Journal of Development Economics.* 136(C), 51–70.

INCLUSIVE AND SUSTAINABLE DEVELOPMENT 79

their families were no longer pursuing more and more years of schooling.[50] Taken together these findings show that caste is a persistent mechanism for exclusion. Affirmative action policies have made some difference over the past few decades which goes to show that state interventions can work. However, the complexities of intersectionality in which reservations benefit a sub-group within a sub-caste while failing to support others, or in which gains in one domain (schooling) fail to translate into another (employment) for historically marginalized groups shows how fine-tuned policy making must be for it to be truly inclusive.

Caste shapes a person's life chances in significant material ways. It further delimits the social spaces a person can move through and the forms of social capital they can access. Here, the denial of rights of entry to dominant caste homes, places of worship, indications of disgust at the touch of a person, and condemnation of eating habits are harms of social regard.[51] These forms of exclusion and discrimination leave deep and lasting scars.[52] They are also the kinds of social exclusion that are challenging to quantify and measure in a development intervention. And yet, these insults to dignity are a form of discrimination and deprivation that cannot be ignored by development practitioners. Finally, it is important to note that, "modern caste persists in the age of the market because of its advantages—its discriminations are opportunities for others, although rarely examined as such."[53] That is, caste is a system of exploitation and advantage for dominant caste groups.

In addition to class, gender, and caste, we could consider how outcomes and opportunities vary by religion, urban/rural location, disability status, region, and language. Rather than going through each one, I want to highlight a few characteristics that are evident even with the three axes of identity discussed so far. First, no axis of identity exists in isolation from the others. That is, each form of social exclusion is linked to others and they often reinforce one another. This quality of intersectionality or interpenetration of the dimensions of identity means that reducing deprivation in one sphere is likely to require

---

50 Jeffrey, Craig, Roger Jeffrey, and Patricia Jeffrey. 2004. "Degrees without Freedom: The Impact of Formal Education on Dalit Young Men in North India." *Development and Change*. 35(5), 963–986.

51 Human Rights Watch. 2007 "Hidden Apartheid: Caste Discrimination against India's 'Untouchables'" Available at https://www.hrw.org/report/2007/02/12/hidden-apartheid/caste-discrimination-against-indias-untouchables#2873 (accessed July 2022).

52 Dutt, Yashica. 2019. *Coming Out as Dalit* New Delhi: Aleph Books.

53 Mosse, David. 2018. "Caste and Development: Contemporary Perspectives on a Structure of Discrimination and Advantage" *World Development*. 110, 422–436.

80 CORPORATE SOCIAL RESPONSIBILITY AND CIVIL SOCIETY

attention to some others as well. The fact that they are mutually reinforcing means that changing power dynamics in one sphere is likely to challenge them in others. Social change is disruptive which means that it generates opposition and backlash. Second, there is considerable variation in life experience within each identity group as people within it are also differentially shaped by their other aspects of identity. That means that interventions that work for some members of a group may not be effective for others. Social change will likely be uneven and happen at different rates for people within any category. Third, material deprivation and social exclusion are deeply intertwined. That means that resolving issues of poverty and material inequality requires attention to social norms and discrimination. What often hurts most is the way that a lack of resources translates into an inability to participate in the social life of a community.[54] It also means that the harms of social exclusion and the gains of inclusion are not measured in caloric intake, wealth, and years of schooling alone. We also must consider the subjective lived experience of the marginalized and their own changing aspirations and goals to document advances.

Macro-structures

Besides the socially constructed norms and hierarchies that shape the horizon of possibility for people in India, the broader structural forces of colonialism and capitalism as well as the historical legacy of certain public policy priorities by the Indian state also matter. What follows is a brief contextualizing sketch of Indian economic history.

Colonial Era

Chapter 1 described the creation of corporations and how they turbo-charged wealth accumulation. "The circuit of commodity circulation was completed via the metropolis where colonial agriculture was linked to metropolitan industry, or colonial consumer goods industry (if and when it was allowed to develop) with metropolitan goods industry; the multiplier effect of these exchanges were thus transmitted abroad."[55] In short, while Britain developed its own industrial infrastructure it demanded Indian raw materials at such low prices that the UK could engage in surplus accumulation. Some have argued

---

54 Scott, James C. 1985. *Weapons of the Weak: Everyday Forms of Peasant Resistance.* New Haven, CT: Yale University Press.
55 Mukherjee, A. 2008. The Return of the Colonial in Indian Economic History: The Last Phase of Colonialism in India. *Social Scientist.* 36(3/4), 3–44.

INCLUSIVE AND SUSTAINABLE DEVELOPMENT   81

that the British actually laid the foundation for later growth in the Indian economy that would not have happened in the absence of colonial rule.[56] The two World Wars forced some decoupling of the Indian economy from global production and consumption, leading to the start of import substitution and the stimulation of domestic consumer industries. As the British decreased the manufacturing interdependence of the two places, they opted for greater financial drain from India to the UK through taxes on imports and exports.[57] Colonialism by definition is about the exploitation of one economy for the benefit of another and the British colonization of India resulted in stunted industry, a lack of investment in agricultural infrastructure, and the absence of domestic financial capital.

Post-independence Period

In 1947, the government of India passed into the hands of the Congress party. The party was led by a Fabian socialist—Nehru, who was deeply influenced by his teacher M. K. Gandhi who argued for an embrace of subsistence agriculture as the path to a self-reliant India. Torn between the desire to modernize India and the need to maintain a fragile political unity the leadership attempted a gradual revolution.[58] The government invested in the development of heavy industry, particularly the domestic production of steel, machinery, and chemicals. This was done in order to make the Indian economy self-reliant, because they believed that the manufacturing sector would produce surplus capital and mass employment, and Indian agricultural yields were quite low as compared to the rest of the world. Investment into public sector enterprises was seen as necessary for India to catch up in economic development.[59] The state was understood to be the main actor in the economy and its roles went beyond planning and regulation to managing prices, production, and distribution of a wide variety of goods. To give these infant industries, a chance to grow and compete globally, trade protections were adopted that cut Indian consumers off from most global supply chains. To staff heavy industry and engage in technology-driven growth, the state invested quite heavily in higher education—particularly technical education.

---

56 Roy, Tirthankar. 2020. *The Economic History of India, 1857–2010*, 4th Edition Oxford, UK: Oxford University Press.
57 Mukherjee, A. 2008. The Return of the Colonial in Indian Economic History: The Last Phase of Colonialism in India. *Social Scientist.* 36(3/4), 3–44.
58 Frankel, Francine. 2006. *India's Political Economy: The Gradual Revolution (1947–2004).*
59 Adhia, Nimisha. 2015. "The History of Economic Development in India since Independence." *Education About Asia.* Association for Asian Studies. 20(3), (Winter).

The result of these policies was a relatively slow rate of growth in the economy, stagnation in agriculture, and the creation of a few huge industrial houses alongside millions of mom-and-pop shops but hardly any mid-sized businesses. One big transformation happened in the late 1960s with the introduction of the "Green Revolution" crops and farming practices which brought new technologies to bear on Indian agriculture. From 1947 to 1967, annual food production was unchanged at 296 kg per person. The adoption of Green Revolution technology led to growth in food production to 365 kg per person by the early 1970s. Annual production of food has now reached 683 kg per person thanks to industrial fertilizers, pesticides, increased mechanization of farming, and GMO seeds.[60] However, this industrial efficiency brings with it problems of environmental pollution, farmer reliance on a cash economy and associated debt burdens, and a reduction in agricultural employment.

In the past decade, scholarship has moved from this narrative, which attributed most of the successes and failures of the Indian economy to national state policies to examine sub-national variation among India's state. Most powerfully, Aseema Sinha has argued that "[...] the Indian state is a divided leviathan; its regional states' actions have surprising and powerful consequences."[61] Regional bureaucracies and micro institutions respond to central directives quite differently and are the implementing agencies. Their adherence to or resistance to federal policies is key to variation in outcomes in economic performance in India. Today, India shows huge discrepancies between its states in economic development. The small state of Goa boasts a per capita GDP that is ten times that of sprawling Bihar. By comparison, the US's richest state (New York) is only double its poorest state (Mississippi).[62] Sub-national government clearly matters.

Post-liberalization

While since 1980, India has experienced durable and continuous growth, concerns remain about the patterns of economic development. These are, "a structural transformation that has skipped high-productivity manufacturing despite surplus labor [sic], an increased spatial divergence in income despite integration in internal markets, limited convergence in education and other

---

60 Chand, R. and J. Singh. 2023. "From Green Revolution to Amrit Kaal" *Niti Aayog Working Paper 02/2023*, GOI. Available at https://www.niti.gov.in/sites/default/files/2023-07/Aggricultrue_Amritkal.pdf (accessed September 2023).

61 Sinha, Aseema. 2015. *The Regional Roots of Developmental Politics in India: A Divided Leviathan*. Bloomington, IN: Indiana University Press.

62 *The Economist*. 2022. "Latitude is Everything" Oct 27.

social metrics across castes but divergence across religions, a deep societal preference for sons that is associated with poor outcomes for women and high levels of stunting amongst children, and an environmental degradation that is severe for its level of income."[63] The gap between population and employment growth, the uneven distribution of human capital (education, health) and the pressure on the ecosystem leave India's gains in raising incomes quite vulnerable to social and political conflict.

The 1980s was a period of slow but steady growth in the Indian economy with some important decisions made during the government of Rajiv Gandhi such as the relative deregulation of the informational technology sector and decentralization of politics and policymaking to more local levels of government. These decisions bore fruit in the following decades with India being an early producer of computing and internet services which integrated the Indian service sector with the global economy. The political decentralization and affirmative action for municipal and village governing bodies helped usher in many new entrants into electoral politics, including millions of women and oppressed castes and tribes. The research on women in local governance suggests they are less corrupt, focus more on human development investments, and are less likely to serve narrow interests.[64]

Other aspects of economic development also show the continuing impact of social identity on policymaking and growth-related outcomes. In Murali's work, she identifies how the particular political coalitions in various states shape their post-1991 industrial policy in ways that emphasize either growth or redistribution concerns. "Narrow capitalist" coalitions comprising a few socially and economically dominant castes with significant business representation are most likely to create pro-business policy frames. The "narrow-poor" electoral base made up of oppressed caste groups and with marginal business presence, maximizes redistribution and doesn't pursue business-friendly policies. The wide coalitions—both poor and capitalist— face contradictory demands and show variation in their policies based on the degree of business representation.[65]

Liberalization of the Indian economy in 1991 marked a significant break with older economic policies. Liberalization began as a series of fiscal reforms

---

63 Lamba, Rohit, and Arvind Subramanian. 2020. "Dynamism with Incommensurate Development: The Distinctive Indian Model." *Journal of Economic Perspectives*. 34(1), 3–30.

64 Saxena, Anupama. 2023. "Women representatives in India" Panel discussion organised by SNDT University, Mumbai. October 3, 2023.

65 Murali, K. 2017. *Caste, Class, and Capital: The Social and Political Origins of Economic Policy in India.* Cambridge: Cambridge University Press. doi:10.1017/9781316659007.

84   CORPORATE SOCIAL RESPONSIBILITY AND CIVIL SOCIETY

to address a balance of payments crisis in 1991 but went on to become, "A wide-ranging reformulation of the relationship between economy and state [...]"[66] Liberalization involved the deregulation of companies, lifting restrictions on foreign trade and investment, and the entry of private business into previously state-run sectors like education, telecommunications, sanitation, healthcare, and energy production. Gupta and Sivaramakrishnan argue that liberalization and decentralization have led to fast growth, deeper inequality among regions, reductions in poverty, and greater complexity in how citizens access the state. The provision and expansion of welfare provisions in the 2000s was interpreted by Partha Chatterjee as evidence that the state was actively staving off class warfare. As liberalization alienated the peasantry and urban proletariat from their means of livelihood, the state stepped in to provide minimal services.[67] Others point to the role of political mobilization in demanding specific rights and support as more important.[68] Either way, liberalization in India is regarded as a new phase in economic development, unlike any previous mode.

Looking back on the past half century of economic development in India, two failures and two successes stand out. The failures are a lack of investment in primary education and basic health; essentially a shortfall in developing human capital.[69] The successes are the reduction in poverty, and second, the gains in gender equality over the past decade discussed above. The distribution of resources, opportunities, and policy benefits is always uneven. Deciding what and who to favor and even who is forgotten in the policymaking process are all political decisions. Therefore, the outcomes of deprivation, opulence, and equality are all politically determined—what varies is how explicit and intentional the decision-making process is. In the absence of conscious choices to be inclusive and sustainable, policies will support or cause exclusion and resource exploitation.

The present is a time of rapid growth and the uneven distribution of the benefits of this growth. Perhaps for the first time, India is in a position

---

66 Gupta, Akhil and Kalyanakrishnan Sivaramakrishnan, (Eds.). 2011. *The State in India after Liberalization: Interdisciplinary Perspectives.* London, UK: Routledge.
67 Chatterjee, P. 2008. "Democracy and Economic Transformation in India." *Economic and Political Weekly.* 43(16), 53–62.
68 Ruparelia, S. 2013. "India's New Rights Agenda: Genesis, Promises, Risks." *Pacific Affairs.* 86(3), 569–590.
69 Pande, Arpana. 2020. *Making India Great.* New York, NY: Harper Collins; Krishnan, Ravi. 2015. "Why India's Health System Needs an Overhaul" *Mint* Dec 14. Available at https://www.livemint.com/Opinion/qXD81719wXXDQVpGyyARrO/Seven-charts-that-show-why-Indias-healthcare-system-needs-a.html (accessed September 2020).

to end poverty and bring its economy onto a sustainable and inclusive path. It is also a time when political decisions will either make this happen or prevent it from being realized. This section considers the role of various sectors in helping to make development sustainable and inclusive. The least likely source of inclusive and sustainable development support is international actors who set the terms of global economic activity. The market is amoral-it does not select for or avoid particular outcomes but it can be directed toward certain goals through persuasion or regulation. State actors are accountable to the people through elections and have a variety of tools at their disposal to shape development pathways. Finally, civil society is the realm that is most dependent on reflecting the views and needs of ordinary people as their support is the chief currency for civil society legitimacy and relevance. Therefore it is the most likely to push for more inclusive and sustainable development priorities.

India, along with other Global South states, has been a rule taker not a rule maker,[70] in the international economy. The basic architecture of the global economy was created in the aftermath of WWII in ways that preserved colonial practices of relying on the Global South for the production and extraction of raw materials and the Global North for financial capital and manufacturing. The Bretton Woods institutions and their disproportionate weight to the minority of wealthy states have proven to be a barrier to the economic development of the Global South. Changing certain rules and practices could make a big difference in achieving more inclusive and sustainable growth. Among them are a relaxation of intellectual property rights protections,[71] eliminating tax havens,[72] forgiving loan repayments,[73] reducing agricultural subsidies,[74] and fully funding climate change mitigation efforts.[75] These would leave global capitalism in place but make it fairer and

---

70 Kripalani, Manjeet. (Ed.). 2021. *India in the G20 Rule-taker to Rule-maker.* Routledge India: New Delhi.

71 Oberthür, Sebastian et al. 2011 "Intellectual Property Rights on Generic Resources and the Fight against Poverty." European Parliament, Brussels. Available at https://www.ecologic.eu/11982 (accessed September 2022).

72 Shaxson, N. 2018. *The Finance Curse: How Global Finance is Making Us All Poorer* Vintage: London, UK.

73 Jensen, Lars. 2022. "Avoiding 'Too Little Too Late' on International Debt Relief" *UNDP* Available at https://www.undp.org/publications/dfs-avoiding-too-little-too-late-international-debt-relief (accessed October 2023).

74 FAO, UNDP and UNEP. 2021. "A multi-billion-dollar opportunity – Repurposing agricultural support to transform food systems." Rome, FAO. https://doi.org/10.4060/cb6562en.

75 Bhattacharya, Amar, Richard Calland, Alina Averchenkova, Lorena Gonzales, Leonardo Martinez-Diaz, Jerome Van Rooij. 2020. "Delivering on the $100 Billion

86   CORPORATE SOCIAL RESPONSIBILITY AND CIVIL SOCIETY

more inclusive. More radical forms of change could involve reparations[76] and the imposition of globally redistributive taxes[77] as well as a move away from growth-oriented economic activity.[78]

Looking at the role of the Indian state, we can again identify a series of policies that could enhance inclusivity and sustainability. Fully funding and implementing the various welfare schemes like the National Food Security Act, Forest Rights Act, Right to Information, National Rural Employment Guarantee Act, Right to Education Act, and so on would keep the state's promises to the most vulnerable citizens. There are dozens of these rights and provisions that offer support to the poor, but they are regularly criticized for corruption, lack of implementation, or redundancy. Instead, some suggest that the introduction of a universal basic income is the most direct path to eliminating poverty.[79] Others (like the conservatives at The Economist) argue that providing cash assistance to everyone except the top 25% is an even more effective approach.[80] The massive reduction in poverty in the past decade is the result of better nutrition, more years of schooling, improved sanitation, and access to cleaner cooking fuels.[81] Each of these improvements grows out of specific state initiatives to meet the basic needs of the people. And the Niti Aayog report shows that the greatest reductions are taking place in the states with the worst indicators which suggests that these interventions are reaching those who need them the most. In addition to these universal interventions and supports, actions to reassure embattled

---

Climate Finance Commitment" Available at https://www.un.org/sites/un2.un.org/files/2020/12/100_billion_climate_finance_report.pdf (accessed October 2023).

76 Lukka, Priya. 2020. "Can reparations help us to re-envision international development?" *Open Democracy* Available at https://www.opendemocracy.net/en/transformation/can-reparations-help-us-re-envision-international-development/.

77 Chancel, L., T. Piketty, E. Saez, G. Zucman et al. "World Inequality Report 2022," World Inequality Lab Available at https://wir2022.wid.world/ (accessed October 2023).

78 Jensen, Liselotte. 2023. "Beyond Growth: Pathways Towards Sustainable Prosperity in the EU" European Parliamentary Research Service Available at https://www.europarl.europa.eu/RegData/etudes/STUD/2023/747108/EPRS_STU(2023)747108_EN.pdf (accessed October 2023).

79 Kumar, Virender and Shivani Kanojia. 2017. "The Idea of Basic Income in India: An Analysis." *Business Analyst*. 38(2), 209–226.

80 The Economist. 2019. "The Beauty of Breadth" *The Economist* April 6.

81 Niti Aayog. 2023. "India: National Multidimensional Poverty Index Progress Review" Government of India and UNDP. Available at https://niti.gov.in/sites/default/files/2023-08/India-National-Multidimentional-Poverty-Index-2023.pdf (accessed October 2023).

religious minorities[82] and the repeal of laws that grant immunity to the armed forces[83] or those that allow the state to detain suspects on flimsy grounds[84] would reduce the fear and exclusion that too many Indians live under today. Finally, the state could stop favoring certain businessmen and their projects over the needs of the public, especially the indigenous groups whose land and resources are often most subject to exploitation and pollution.[85] These steps would put the increasingly effective resources of the state to work for all Indians in pursuit of more inclusive and sustainable development.

The private sector in India of course is a major driver of economic growth. Besides its core function of producing goods and services, some believe the private sector can serve as a model for social inclusion through corporate social responsibility initiatives and as a participant in policy design.[86] And finally, the private sector and its wealth is increasingly being tapped into for philanthropic work. Business activity is also the prime contributor to a range of negative externalities in terms of pollution,[87] overuse of natural resources, and the creation of a consumerist mindset. Rather than thinking of what business can do to guide the social sector or what already wealthy individuals can do in terms of philanthropy, the private sector can have its greatest impact by shifting its core business practices.[88] By adopting more sustainable practices in terms of production, by internalizing the true costs of production, and by eschewing advertising to create want, business could become part of the solution to the challenges of deprivation and inequality.

---

82 Khurshid, Salman. 2019. *Visible Muslim, Invisible Christian.* Rupa: New Delhi, India.

83 Mc-Duie Ra, Duncan. 2009. *Contemporary South Asia: Special Issue* Vol 17:3.

84 Sebastian, John and Faiza Rahman. 2023. "Improving Preventative Detention Laws" *The India Forum* May 15. Available at https://www.theindiaforum.in/law/improving-preventive-detention-laws (accessed October 2023).

85 Hindenburg Research. 2023. "Adani Group: How the World's 3rd Richest Man is Pulling the Largest Con in Corporate History" January 24. Available at https://hindenburgresearch.com/adani/ (accessed June 2023).

86 Nelson, Jane. 2006. "Leveraging the Development Impact of Business in the Fight Against Global Poverty" *Corporate Social Responsibility Initiative Working Paper 22* Cambridge, MA: Harvard University and Mulky, Avinash. 2017. "Are CSR activities directed towards SDGs? A study in India" *OEFL Conference on Governance, Management and Entrepreneurship,* Dubrovnik: Croatia.

87 Gupta, A. and D. Spears. 2017. "Health Externalities of India's Expansion of Coal Plants: Evidence from a National Panel of 40,000 Households." *Journal of Environmental Economic Management.* November, 86, 262–276.

88 Medina-Munoz, Rita D. and Diego R. Medina-Munoz. 2019. "Corporate Social Responsibility for Poverty Alleviation: An Integrated Research Framework." *Business Ethics.* 2020(20), 3–19.

88 CORPORATE SOCIAL RESPONSIBILITY AND CIVIL SOCIETY

Finally, civil society can play some role in designing a more inclusive and sustainable India. The greatest strength of civil society organizations is their deep knowledge of and ongoing responsiveness to various publics. They are embedded within particular communities or localities and have social and professional networks that connect them to many people. There is a huge need for accurate and meaningful data to understand deprivation and inequality as well as to identify effective interventions that ameliorate it.[89] They are more likely to ask the right questions and identify the priorities of the people that anti-poverty and social inclusion measures are supposed to aid. Often, frontline workers in CSOs come from the very families or communities the CSO serves. Their professionalization within the CSO world builds their skills and capacity to offer translation of needs and preferences into a language that is legible to policymakers. This means that CSOs are often in a good position to conduct research, especially participatory research into the needs of specific groups. They can also serve as representatives who are bicultural in that they can belong to a community but also have the skills to move within policymaking and advocacy spaces. After all, the best way to solve the problems of deprivation is to follow the lead of those who experience it themselves.[90]

CSOs are also often responsible for engaging in advocacy on behalf of marginalized groups. They may identify a particular need that was previously unrecognized. By framing it as a political problem they can demand a response or action on it. In their framing, they may prompt certain types of action or policy to be adopted. When there are conflicting interests and goals, while the powerful have access to the state through personal networks and official channels, CSOs can use grassroots mobilization to demand a seat at the table for the weaker sections. Finally, one of the most important functions of civil society as a whole is to provide democratic accountability. That is, by describing conditions on the ground, articulating the demands of the people, and pointing out the gaps between political promises and policy implementation they pressure the state to account for itself. In addition to the pressure they bring to bear on the state, civil society also offers space for the imagination of and development of alternative visions for economic development and political community. These debates and visions remind us that there are multiple possibilities before us and that we are always choosing a path—it is up to us to do so mindfully.

---

89 Banerjee, Abjijit and Esther Duflo. 2011. *Poor Economics*. New York: Public Affairs.
90 Deveaux, M. 2018. Poor-Led Social Movements and Global Justice. *Political Theory*. 46(5), 698–725.

INCLUSIVE AND SUSTAINABLE DEVELOPMENT   89

This chapter describes sustainable and inclusive development as an approach that extends time horizons and widens the scope of who and what is considered a relevant stakeholder in human activities. The ideal of sustainability is a growth process that considers the economy, the environment, and society, including future society. Inclusive development focuses on marginalized people and asks if growth is the appropriate goal of economic activity. It also nudges decisionmakers to ask systemic and normative questions as they chart development agendas.

Thinking about what sustainable and inclusive development requires allows us to turn our attention to the quality and origins of deprivation. I specifically show that poverty is a lack of resources and a denial of dignity. It is defined by a combination of material deprivation and social exclusion. Poverty is a social condition not just a material condition. Development must address the social and psychological dimensions of deprivation, exploitation, and exclusion. In the Indian context, inclusivity means addressing the social bases of exclusion. Gender, sexuality, class, disability, region, religion, and caste are all factors that predict a person's degree of inclusion or exclusion in Indian political, economic, and social life. The chapter provides an overview of poverty, class, gender, caste, and religious identities.

In describing the varieties of exclusion and deprivation that makeup India's pattern of resource and status distribution, I show that many of these identity categories are interlinked. That is, inequality in one dimension rests upon inequality in another. That means that undoing exploitation and oppression requires a messy, holistic transformation rather than a narrow technocratic approach. For instance, the patriarchal control over women's reproductive abilities is crucial to ensuring endogamous marriages are the norm in Indian society, and thus maintains caste boundaries. The connection between gender roles within the family and most other forms of exclusion in India shows how intersectionality shows up. Inclusion requires transformation of multiple spheres of identity and action simultaneously.

Then I turn to an examination of the causes of inequality by tracing the evolution of India's political economy through history as well as in relation to the global economy, as well as examining a variety of social norms that are relevant. I describe the colonial period, the early democratic socialism of the independence era, the populist era, the neoliberal reform period, and today's crony capitalism. The distribution of resources, opportunities, and policy benefits is always uneven. Policies determine who is deprived, opulent, and equal, and how explicit and intentional the decision-making process is. Not choosing is not an option.

Finally, the chapter concludes by considering what role international actors, the Indian state, corporations, and civil society can play in sustainable

90   CORPORATE SOCIAL RESPONSIBILITY AND CIVIL SOCIETY

and inclusive development. The least likely source of inclusive and sustainable development support is international actors, the market is amoral, but state actors are accountable to the people through elections, and civil society is most dependent on reflecting the views of ordinary people. Therefore, I suggest that the most likely source of improvements in the lives of most Indians are likely to be driven by policy interventions by the state and through the advocacy and accountability that CSOs can provide. I suggest that it is doubtful that corporations or international actors can or will be major players in making economic activity work for the many.

Chapter 4

CORPORATE PROMISE AND REALITY

To expect the powerful to question the legitimacy of the system in which they gained their power would be a utopian absurdity.[1]

The promise of a partnership is to bring together two entities with varying strengths so they can increase their impact, learn from each other, and achieve things that neither could do individually. The way that incentives are set up in the Indian laws governing CSR, the most frequent type of CSR partnership is one of a corporation funding an implementing agency (usually a CSO) to carry out a program. However, as the CSR sector matures, increasingly companies are staffing their CSR offices with people with development/social sector training and experience who are keen to help create the programs they fund. That is, they increasingly want to move from being just donors to actual implementing partners.

In this chapter, I consider some of the ways in which these cross-sectoral partnerships were theorized and some of the ways in which they have actually played out. The premise of the CSR law is that corporations have some ways of operating that could make the nonprofit world work better. This assumption is broken down into its components and compared to the reality of corporate–CSO partnerships. The chapter concludes with some reflections on social entrepreneurship—an organizational form that embodies the promise of corporate approaches to solving social problems.

As an example, in 2013 as the Companies Act was being finalized, Ernst and Young released a study with their analysis and predictions about the future of CSR in India. They suggested that the state stepping in to provide some guidelines would lead to greater coordination and strategic use of CSR to make business more sustainable. They anticipated a win–win situation for all. They anticipated benefits for industry, development beneficiaries,

---

1 Rieff, David. 2015. *The Reproach of Hunger: Food, Justice, and Money in the Twenty-first Century.* New York, NY: Simon & Schuster.

and the state with their only concerns being that CSR may not maximize returns unless it was done strategically. The possibility of it not working well for any other reason is not considered. "The Companies Bill have [sic] opened a new opportunity for all the stakeholders including the corporate sector, government, not for profit organizations and the community at large to evolve innovative ways to synergize efforts and contribute toward equitable social and economical development."[2] They expected that the regulation will blend the best of business in ways that allow them to do well while doing good. Empirical studies of the top 50 or top 500 companies in India and their CSR activity tend to show that the 2013 CSR law has brought more companies into the anti-poverty sector but that the impact of their interventions is mixed at best in actually improving the quality of life of most Indians.[3]

The founder of a consultancy that connects corporations and CSOs explained how the 2013 law helped them transition from basically providing communications support to corporations into a research and assessment role. "Though whenever we worked with organizations our idea was that even though we were doing communications we want to sort of be able to move them [corporations] from these onetime projects to more structural, more long-term projects."[4] It was clear to her that the kind of quick interventions most companies wanted to offer as CSR was not going to have a lasting impact. Corporations needed to learn how to make their involvement in social investing actually work for the beneficiaries, not just as a marketing tool. However, that education has not yet happened. She goes on to describe a troubling phenomenon. "I have gone to multiple schools where three organizations [are] doing [the] same sort of things. A lot of waste of resources." Multiple CSOs or corporates offer tutoring to students of a school because of a lack of coordination and planning. She also points out that this kind of replication of effort is most common in the more developed states which is where the most industry is located and the need is the least.

It is also the case that when one looks closely at the annual reports of specific corporations, some of them have indeed engaged in more CSR since 2013. But others have actually reduced their CSR expenditure to the recommended

---

2 Ernst & Young. 2013. "India Inc: Companies Act 2013 An Overview" pp 22 Available at https://www.ey.com/en_in/financial-accounting-advisory-services/companies-act (accessed August 7, 2016).

3 Mulky, Avinash. 2017. "Are CSR activities directed towards SDGs? A study in India" *OEFL Conference on Governance, Management and Entrepreneurship*, Dubrovnik: Croatia and Sarkar, Jayati and Subrata Sarkar. 2015. "CSR in India: An Effort to Bridge the Welfare Gap" *Review of Market Integration.* 7(1).

4 Mulchandani, Payal. 2019. Personal Interview. Mumbai August 26.

CORPORATE PROMISE AND REALITY

two percent. And some continue to fail to meet their required levels. For example, in fiscal year 2013–2014, Reliance Industries was spending 3.24% of annual profits but by 2021–2022, they were down to 2%. Tata Motors went from 5.17% to not reporting any because the company had losses, not profits in 2021–2022. TCS increased from 0.48% to 2.1% as did fellow technology firm Infosys which went from 0.09% to 1.8%. Turning to public sector companies, Indian Oil Corp increased from 1.20% to 2.7% and another oil company, Bharat Petroleum doubled its CSR from 0.85% to 1.6%. Financial services firm, State Bank of India reduced its expenditure from 1.37% to 1%.[5] All of these numbers go to show that there is considerable diversity in how individual corporations responded to Article 135 over the past decade.

Coca-Cola Case Study

One of the world's largest and best-known brands—the Coca-Cola company, collaborating with NDTV, launched a major CSR campaign in 2011 with a 12-hour telethon to raise funds for rural schools in India. Various celebrities spoke in support of the fundraiser, with cricketer Sachin Tendulkar serving as campaign ambassador.[6] This initial phase of the campaign raised about $1.7 million and supported about 270 schools by building better bathrooms, drinking water facilities, and improving playground infrastructure.[7] This was part of Coca-Cola's response to Indian accusations of it depleting water resources, polluting neighboring aquifers, and suppressing investigations into its business practices. A state investigative commission called on Coca-Cola to pay $47 million in damages to the state of Kerala.[8] This fine was never paid. Instead the company paid $2 million to a well-regarded think tank—TERI to conduct an "independent" investigation. The annual profits of Coca-Cola in India range from $50 to $60 million per year in the past decade.[9]

---

5 Annual reports from corporation websites.

6 Mahapatra, S. and Swatantra. 2015. "Support My School." *IOSR Journal of Business and Management*. 1–12.

7 Best Media Info 2013. "Coca Cola NDTV Raises 13.5 crore" Available at https://bestmediainfo.com/2013/02/coca-cola-ndtv-support-my-school-campaign-raises-rs-13-5-crore-for-rural-schools (accessed July 5, 2022).

8 Reuters 2010. "Coca Cola Unit Asked to Pay $47 million in damages" March 23. Available at https://www.reuters.com/article/india-cocacola/coca-cola-india-unit-asked-to-pay-47-million-damages-idUSSGE62M0AV20100323 (accessed July 5, 2022).

9 *The Hindu* 2021. " Coca-Cola India net profit declines 28.4% to ₹443.4 crore in FY21; revenue down 16%" November 21. Available at https://www.thehindu.com/business/Industry/coca-cola-india-net-profit-declines-284-to-4434-crore-in-fy21-revenue-down-16/article37391031.ece (accessed July 5, 2022).

94   CORPORATE SOCIAL RESPONSIBILITY AND CIVIL SOCIETY

While this is a small piece of the global profits of $2–$9 billion, the Indian market is seen as a major growth opportunity because as yet not many of India's millions of potential customers drink bottled drinks.[10]

What is the Support my School initiative? Is it a way to make amends for the harm that the company has caused?[11] Is it a way to contribute to inclusive and sustainable development? Is it a way to rebrand itself? Is it a way to advertise its product and attract new customers? According to one observer,

> The latest is the Coca-Cola India 'Support My school' campaign with NDTV. I like this campaign as it picks a cause that is universal and big. It is about kids and their rights and the need to education. It picks rural and small town schools. It takes valuable resources to the points of need. It is not shy and does not use subterfuge as well. It talks to its audience without resorting to the in-your-face tools of advertising. It helps build future customers. In that way, it gives and takes. It gives resources today to support a nation of school-going children. It takes subliminally. It takes when it impinges its brand name all across, and plants a soft thought of an otherwise hard brand in the minds of impressionable kids.

Bijoor argues that it is ethically sound for companies to engage in CSR initiatives that also improve their bottom line. After all, "organisations must aim at profit in their ventures, both commercial or CSR oriented. However, in making this profit happen, it is not wrong if good money can chase good causes such as this one."[12] But Coca-Cola is not only pursuing the greater good while burnishing its reputation.

Coca-Cola has a history of marketing campaigns designed to mislead various target groups about the health effects of drinking its products.[13] In the Indian

---

10 Fortune Data Store. 2022. "Fortune 500" Available at https://fortune.com/company/coca-cola/fortune500/ (accessed July 5, 2022).

11 Carmichael, B. and C. Moriarty. 2018. "How Coca-Cola Came to terms with its own water crisis" *Washington Post* May 31. Available at https://www.washingtonpost.com/news/business/wp/2018/05/31/how-coca-cola-came-to-terms-with-its-own-water-crisis/ (accessed July 4 2022).

12 Bijoor, H. 2012. "CSR: A marketing tool" Available at https://indiacsr.in/csr-a-marketing-tool/ (accessed July 4, 2022).

13 Wood, B., G. Ruskin, and G. Sacks. 2019. Targeting Children and Their Mothers, Building Allies and Marginalising Opposition: An Analysis of Two Coca-Cola Public Relations Requests for Proposals. *International Journal of Environmental Research and Public Health*, 17(1), 12.

case, they used TERI's credibility to attack the credibility of Sunita Narain's Centre for Science and Environment which conducted the initial research on the harmful environmental effects of Coke's bottling facilities. Despite the fact that the TERI report did not exonerate the company, its PR office declared that TERI had shown it was blameless.[14] This kind of effort reflects a highly sophisticated public relations effort in which the company takes the negative actions it is accused of and very publicly engages in tokenistic acts that give the opposite impression.[15] Thus, it continues to sell a product that no one needs, that has a known negative effect on health, that over-exploits natural resources like water, and it spends as much money on advertising its good works as actually doing them. After years of critical reports by Indian researchers, protests in the streets, and criticism from Indian governments, Coca-Cola adopted a replenishment policy by which they pledged to be at least water neutral.[16] That is, they developed a series of projects to improve water efficiency in their production processes and partnered with a variety of CSOs like WorldVision, WaterAid, and so on to offset their water use by supporting access to clean water around the world. Today, they boast about their water policies and specifically that they have positively impacted 100,000 Indian students.[17] Aneel Karnani examined Coca-Cola's impact on groundwater in Rajasthan where the company promised their rain water harvesting stations were replenishing aquifers at a greater rate than they were withdrawing water. He found there was no evidence to support this claim and good reason to doubt it. "The company is not keeping its own promises." He concluded that corporations are unable to resist over-use of common pool resources and that government regulation is the only way forward.[18]

---

14 Ciafone, A. 2012. "If 'Thanda Matlab Coca-Cola' Then 'Cold Drink Means Toilet Cleaner': Environmentalism of the Dispossessed in Liberalizing India." *International Labor and Working-Class History*, 81, 114–135.

15 For documentation on this see work by Amit Srivastava at the India Resource Center Available at http://www.indiaresource.org/ (accessed July 5, 2022).

16 Grady, B. 2016. "Coca-Cola and its bottlers 'replenish' all the water they use" *Green Biz* August 29. Available at https://www.greenbiz.com/article/coca-cola-and-its-bottlers-replenish-all-water-they-use (accessed July 5, 2022).

17 Coca Cola Company. 2021. "Business and ESG Reports: Water" Available at https://www.coca-colacompany.com/content/dam/journey/us/en/reports/coca-cola-business-environmental-social-governance-report-2021.pdf#page=21 and World Vision 2022. "Corporate Partnerships" Available at https://www.worldvision.org/corporate/partners/coca-cola/ (accessed July 5, 2022).

18 Karnani, Aneel. 2014. "Corporate Social Responsibility Does Not Avert the Tragedy of the Commons. Case Study: Coca-cola India." *Economics, Management, and Financial Markets*. 9(3), 1–23.

96   CORPORATE SOCIAL RESPONSIBILITY AND CIVIL SOCIETY

At the global level, their Water campaign gets good press coverage, but in India to improve sanitation for 100,000 students is a very modest achievement. Based on the 2011 census, India has 315 million students. That means, Coca-Cola reached less than 0.03% of India's students through its CSR. Meanwhile, it is frustrated that the poorest 300 million Indians aren't consuming packaged drinks yet.[19] Of course, this means that about 1 billion Indians have been reached by Coca-Cola as consumers of its beverages. The company donated $173.5 million in total around the world to support charities and communities in 2021, which is 2% of its worldwide revenue.[20] Meanwhile, its global advertising budget is $4.1 billion[21] and its Indian advertising budget is about $63 million.[22]

The Coca-Cola Foundation, which is the charitable arm of the company, dispenses grants to various projects and CSOs around the world. In 2020 in India, it gave about $4.3 million for COVID relief, $1 million for humanitarian relief after natural disasters, $0.32 for water replenishment, $0.53 million for recycling awareness campaigns, and $0.1 million for sanitation.[23] That's a grand total of $6.3 million in charity in India during 2020. Again, its charitable giving is 10% of its advertising budget in India and about 10% of its annual profits in a market that is still in its early stages of development.

Is Coca-Cola a CSR success story or a failure? The advocacy by civil society groups and CSOs in India seems to have led to some shifts in the production processes of the company. The attempt to conserve water and restore watersheds is a great example of what was previously a cost of business externalized to society broadly being internalized by

---

19 Bhushan, R. 2017. "Coca Cola is yet to crack the code" *Economic Times* November 20. Available at https://economictimes.indiatimes.com/industry/cons-products/food/coca-cola-is-yet-to-crack-the-code-in-indian-market/articleshow/61717497.cms?from=mdr (accessed July 4, 2022).

20 Coca Cola Company. 2021. "Business and ESG Reports" Available at https://www.coca-colacompany.com/content/dam/journey/us/en/reports/coca-cola-business-environmental-social-governance-report-2021.pdf#page=21 (accessed July 5, 2022).

21 https://www.statista.com/statistics/286526/coca-cola-advertising-spending-worldwide/ (accessed July 5, 2022)

22 Exchange 4 media. 2021. "Cola Majors Spend on Advertising FY21" November 15. Available at https://www.exchange4media.com/marketing-news/cola-majors-spent-over-rs-900-crore-on-advertising-in-fy21-116840.html (accessed July 6, 2022).

23 Coca Cola Foundation. 2021. "Charitable Contributions Report" Available at https://www.coca-colacompany.com/content/dam/journey/us/en/policies/pdf/the-coca-cola-foundation/2020-charitable-contributions-report.pdf   (accessed July 6, 2022).

CORPORATE PROMISE AND REALITY

the company. However, this did not happen as a result of partnership with CSOs, but thanks to vocal opposition by CSOs to Coca-Cola's business practices. The partnerships with NDTV and other groups in Support our Schools on the other hand seem to be a fairly modest initiative, although it has a high media profile and generated good publicity for the company at a time when its reputation had taken a beating. This actual CSR collaboration has been a success in terms of improving the company's reputation but cannot be credited with achieving very much for rural school students. And the overall goal of the company to transform these rural students into customers who will switch from drinking water or homemade drinks to ones who will pay a premium for the packaged, high calorie drinks sold by Coca-Cola is unchanged. This goal of creating consumers of wasteful and unhealthy drinks is the elephant in the room. Until that core practice is addressed, the CSO vision of a healthy society and the corporate vision of endless growth and consumption remain at odds.

Table Corporation and CSO key characteristics[24]

Characteristics	Corporations	Nonprofit/CSOs
Objectives	Profit	Social benefit
Focus	Immediate customer satisfaction	Long-term improvements
Organizational culture	Resource rich Expenses as investment	Resource scarce Expenses as cost
Target	Customers	Beneficiaries
Performance Measurement	Sales Revenue, ROI, Dividends, Market Share	Clients served, Client satisfaction, Repeat donors
Employees	Paid	Paid and volunteer
Revenue	Sales	Grants, donors, fee for service
Exchange	Money	Free, some participation, some fee
Accountability	Shareholders	Stakeholders
Product	Goods and services	Services, carework, training
Demand	Typically steady	Unpredictable

---

24 Adapted from Chad, P., E. Kyriazis and J. Motion. 2013. "Development of a Market Orientation Research Agenda for the Nonprofit Sector." *Journal of Nonprofit & Public Sector Marketing*. 25, 1–27.

Promises—Efficiency, Innovation, Measurable Results, Capacity

In comparison with the nonprofit sector, there are certain characteristics of the corporate world promoted as superior ways of operating. In addition to their money, these superiorities are what business is supposed to bring to the table in collaborations with CSOs. Bottom-line thinking or a focus on results is a key strength of the corporate approach. The assumption is that nonprofits are not as results driven and are easily distracted by the pet proclivities of their workers. Lacking shareholders, they don't have to deliver results to stay in business. This is a plausible concern in that the operating budget for most CSOs comes from grants and donations rather than from the people to whom they are delivering their "product." Sex workers or migrant laborers may be the target beneficiaries of CSO activities but are not in a position to direct the CSO agenda or to fund its operations. In the corporate world, company owners have invested their capital in the firm and can demand accountability and results.

Looking at the table with key differences between corporations and CSOs, one of the most obvious differences is in terms of how results are measured. Corporations are able to point to an actual rupee or dollar figure to assess how well they are doing their core business from quarter to quarter. CSOs usually don't have such a clear and quantifiable metric they can use to measure their results. And in fact, many CSOs are quite vague about having any observable metrics at all. The introduction of randomized controlled trials in poverty intervention has been such a huge revolution because prior to that most development CSOs didn't make any effort to assess the efficacy of their programs. "Impact evaluation based on randomized controlled trials (RCTs) offers a powerful tool that has fundamentally reshaped development economics by offering novel solutions to long-standing problems of weak causal identification."[25] In fact, Esther Dufflo, Abhijit Banerjee, and Michael Kremer won the 2019 Nobel Prize in Economics for pioneering the use of RCTs in development economics. "The amount of high-quality empirical evidence used in development economics is almost unrecognizable compared with what it was before this revolution took off."[26] They fundamentally changed how policymakers and scholars think about the development process

---

25 Barrett, C. B. and M. R. Carter. 2010. "The Power and Pitfalls of Experiments in Development Economics: Some Non-random Reflections." *Applied Economic Perspectives and Policy*. 32: 515–548.

26 Olken, B. A. 2020. "Banerjee, Duflo, Kremer, and the Rise of Modern Development Economics." *Scandinavian Journal of Economics*. 122, 853–878.

CORPORATE PROMISE AND REALITY 99

and what we can measure about it. There have been a number of criticisms and discussions of the limitations of RCTs, but even critics concede that they have pushed the whole field of development studies to focus on results and measurement in new ways.[27]

CSO accountability is divided in ways that make donors much more powerful than the people the CSO serves.[28] This reflects the power differentials in society—CSOs generally serve the more marginalized and under-resourced groups in society who do not have access to the power or resources to achieve their own goals. The CSO's operational costs and those of the services or goods provided to beneficiaries are paid for by donors who are usually wealthier and more powerful than the CSO itself. The exception to this model are membership-based CSOs which embed accountability in the community they serve, even while fundraising from institutional donors to supplement their own members' contributions. Even those CSOs which routinely engaged in evaluations at the conclusion of their projects, often fail to monitor their impact during the project period.[29]

Since the 1990s, the CSO sector has become increasingly professionalized and some of the early criticisms of a lack of attention to process are no longer as relevant. The introduction of RCTs and their embrace by effective altruists and other major donors has pushed CSOs to design their interventions so they can be assessed using this methodology. Effective altruists believe that in a world of urgent needs and competing approaches to meeting those needs, the most effective aid needs to be identified using rigorous methods that will identify the projects that make the biggest impact. This has tended to bias them towards supporting projects and organizations that have a quantifiable and measurable impact such as the distribution of bed nets in malaria zones. They struggle with how to evaluate a program that changes laws and customs related to women's ownership of land, even though they recognize that such a shift is probably quite significant in raising living standards.[30] The emphasis on measurable results is both a selling point and a drawback of the corporate influence over CSOs. I'll return to this idea in the next section on the Realities of corporate collaboration.

---

27 See the special issue of *World Development* 2020. Volume 127.

28 Banks, N., D. Hulme, and M. Edwards. 2015. "CSOs, States, and Donors Revisited: Still Too Close for Comfort?" *World Development*. 66, 707–718.

29 Eckman, K. 1996. "How CSOs Monitor Projects for Impacts: Results of Recent Research." *Impact Assessment*. 14(3), 241–268.

30 Singer, Peter. 2009. *The Life You Can Save*. New York, NY: Random House.

100   CORPORATE SOCIAL RESPONSIBILITY AND CIVIL SOCIETY

Efficiency is another key promise of the corporate sector which often sees itself as nimble and consistently driven to reduce costs and maximize revenue. The assumption is that the corporate sector is adept at identifying opportunities and maximizing the benefits of any investment. This is contrasted with the social sector which is seen as inefficient, caught up in slow decision-making, and with competing imperatives that pull the organization in different directions and this divided attention can make CSOs less efficient.

> Businesses bring in know-how on products that are sometimes highly technical, with a whole logistical setup and broad experience in marketing and distribution. But they rarely know how to reach the poorest population groups. Conversely, CSOs know how to work with economically insecure groups and how to listen to their needs, but they often lack resources. Consequently, their actions are often limited. The complementarity is therefore obvious, and indeed essential if we want to have an impact on populations that are currently cut off from access to vital goods and services. The consequence of these partnerships is, certainly, that the social acceptability of the business is reinforced. But so is the reputation of the CSO regarding its impact and effectiveness.[31]

The technical and efficiency focus of a business can advance the work of an CSO that is skilled at connecting with the most marginalized but is not particularly efficient at delivering resources on its own.

In a related vein, collaborations are also supposed to bring increased capacity in scope for the CSO and more access for the business. "When they work well these partnerships can provide companies with new challenges, fresh ideas, added credibility and better reach into communities, customers and government. For the CSO they can provide further resources, and the ability to reach more people, new skills and increased capacity."[32] In this formulation, we have win–win outcomes from collaboration. The staid world of nonprofits will be energized and improved by corporate partnerships. And the soulless world of corporations will be humanized and connected to people through their work with CSOs.

---

31 Ménascé, D. 2016. "CSO-Business Partnerships: A Win-Win Model- Interview with Franck Renaudin, Founder and Executive Director, Entrepreneurs du Monde." *Field Actions Science Reports*. 14.

32 Restorick, T. 2011. "CSOs and big business can make a partnership of winners" *The Guardian* July 22.

Realities of Corporate–CSO Partnerships

"The inherent differences in mission, governance, strategy and structure between corporations and CSOs mean that business models emanating from their collaborations will usually be opportunistic, project-based initiatives, as opposed to representing deep and fundamental transformational change at the corporate level."[33] The realities of corporate and CSO collaborations are variable. Some partnerships are deep and transformational for both organizations while others are short and superficial engagements meant to insure minimal compliance with the law. However, there are some patterns identified by CSO activists as they try to work with corporate partners that seem quite common and also quite problematic. The goals of nonprofits and corporate firms are very different. Their ways of operating and record keeping are not as divergent, but they reflect varying environments and goals. And when these organizations come together in partnership, their collaborations often look like patronage relationships in which business priorities drive the work at the expense of nonprofit wishes.

Incompatible Time Horizons

In the development sector, community-based organizations have struggled with the challenge of managing donor expectations for programs in terms of their time horizons.[34] A great deal of this tension is based on donor's attempts to insure accountability for the money they are disbursing. They want to know that it is being used effectively. But in order to know this, they end up imposing artificial constraints on development interventions. One of the most common constraints is seen in time boundaries. Most donors have grant cycles of a year, three-year, or maybe a five-year period. Social and economic transformation on the ground requires much longer. First, a CSO must enter a community, build trust and rapport with residents, ascertain their needs, build its capacity to meet those needs, experiment with methodology, gradually scale up its interventions, and overcome unexpected obstacles. How long it takes to build the relationships that undergird most development interventions varies by location and by the type of intervention proposed. Anything that is designed to change existing power dynamics (e.g., women's empowerment) not only

---

33 Dahan, N., J. Doh, J. Oetzel, and M. Yaziji. 2010. "Corporate-CSO Collaboration: Co-creating New Business Models for Developing Market." *Long Range Planning.* 43(10), 326–342.
34 Banks, N., D. Hulme, and M. Edwards. 2015. "CSOs, States, and Donors Revisited: Still Too Close for Comfort?" *World Development.* 66, 707–718.

102   CORPORATE SOCIAL RESPONSIBILITY AND CIVIL SOCIETY

takes longer but also has a greater long-term impact. Fieldworkers will tell you these transformational interventions require decades of trust and support.[35] Where traditional donors have a 3–5-year time horizon, corporate partners are often looking for results in less than a year.

> When corporates want a result, it's okay, what is the outcome? Where will we be in three months, say six months of ever a year, outcome is desired. But then CSOs say we can't bring out a change in one year or six months. We need a period of at least 5 or say 10 years to get a noticeable change in the community's lifestyle [...]. So you have both kinds of things planned into one project, so that corporates get their something noticeable so in terms of things like infra or small things here and there and then you the larger chance—it requires many years to come across.[36]

The rush to produce measurable results in time for an annual report or a filing with the government on CSR programs is simply incompatible with the longer time horizons required to engage in transformational social work.

Lack of Transparency

One of the challenges for CSR collaborations with CSOs among populations that have a history of conflict with the company is the extent to which corporate sponsorship can be a deterrent to engagement. That is, in some cases, the bad reputation and behavior of the company means that when people find out that a CSO is in partnership with the company, they reject the development projects that otherwise were welcomed by the community. This is what happened in a tribal area of Jharkhand with ACC cement and their implementing CSO partner.[37] In one incident, a board was added to a water-tank project being built on private land which listed not only the CSO logo but also the corporate logo of ACC. This was the first time the landowner and other villagers had discovered this CSR project was being sponsored by the company. "Upon sighting the corporate logo on the display

---

35 OECD. 2003. "Harmonising Donor Practices for Effective Aid Delivery" Available at https://www.oecd.org/development/effectiveness/20896122.pdf (accessed August 5, 2022).

36 Agarwal, Radhika. 2015. Personal interview with Deputy Manager of Essar Foundation, Mumbai India.

37 This account relies on an excellent dissertation by Utkarsh Kumar "Mining, CSR, and the Politics of Attrition" 2018 University of Delhi.

CORPORATE PROMISE AND REALITY 103

board, the enraged owner Chumbru,[38] angrily picked up a boulder lying near his foot and smashed the brightly coloured tin-sheet display." It turns out that ACC and Chumbru's family had been in a protracted battle over land rights and he would never have agreed to the project if he had known the truth about the CSR partnership.

At the same inauguration event, male villagers abused local women who had joined the self-help groups organized by the CSO. "They were particularly disgruntled with the CSO staff for concealing the fact of corporate funding by ACC. The village people were fearful that the company might take over their lands by fooling them on the pretext of company funded community development activities." The CSO and the company had concealed their partnership in order to gain trust among the villagers who had already been harmed by the mining company over many decades. Rather than improving the image of the company, this deceit undermined the legitimacy of the CSO. But without the deceit it is unlikely any of these projects would have been possible.

Flexibility in Accounting

In the name of accountability and transparency, corporate donors end up imposing reporting requirements that undermine the ability of CSOs to respond flexibly to realities in the field. This has been a challenge documented over decades and while some foundations[39] have adjusted their practices in recognition of this challenge, most government donors, and now corporations, do not offer much flexibility in accounting practices. One child right's CSO worker, Sonali, said that their organization is one of the few in India to have multiple corporate partners. "Because now there is so much red tape when dealing with corporates and you know the bigger the corporate, the more bureaucracy and all that kind of stuff."[40] Nonprofit workers know that the disciplinary tactics of reporting requirements are highly effective taskmasters. Just as students study for the test, CSOs learn what is required in reports to satisfy funders. Those requirements can easily overcome their own insights and wisdom about what is required by the people they are serving. This agenda capture is achieved through what Bachrach and Baratz

---

38 This is a pseudonym.

39 For example, Co-Impact and Ford Foundation have moved away from Calls for proposals in response to priorities set by Foundation Staff, to more open grant making approaches.

40 "Sonali" and "Latha" are pseudonyms for workers at a child rights CSO. Personal interview with Eamon Malone over phone April 25, 2018.

104   CORPORATE SOCIAL RESPONSIBILITY AND CIVIL SOCIETY

call the "mobilization of bias" which is quiet and avoids any open conflict or confrontation.[41] Quietly, by structuring reports in a particular way, the corporate partner can dominate the collaboration.

Another CSO that works in rural areas reports, "The corporate[s] work more professionally, paper paperwork like documentation, accounting etc. Individual donors are more versatile and liberal to modify, revise the projects as and when it is necessary."[42] Their experience is that corporate donors are more rigid and bureaucratic in their partnerships than individual philanthropists or even the government which is notorious for being bureaucratic. The inability to adapt programs in response to developments on the ground means that CSOs are forced to continue with interventions that are suboptimal or even cause harm to their relationship with the community. Corporate partners have to learn to trust their implementing agencies and recognize that unlike the production of widgets, in social relationships adaptability and flexibility are necessary virtues. The reporting requirements of Article 135 and the threat of criminal or civil legal action taken against CSR officials make extending this trust much harder.

By the Numbers

The impact/result orientation of corporations is part of what explains their concentration in health and education fields where an organization can report, "this many students in tutoring service, with this percentage rise in their end of year scores" or "this many patients given anti-diarrhea medications over a six month period." These examples are of necessary and important interventions and selected to show how some types of work can be quantified. One training organization explained, "[...] we attract corporates only because of our own approach of being very output, outcome and impact driven and I think that is what appeals to corporates. We have very hard numbers on the numbers of students we have enrolled, the number who have completed, the number whom we have placed, so it's all very very concrete."[43] While some programs are the kind that can be quantified, even advocates

---

41 Bachrach, P., and M. S. Baratz. 1962. "Two Faces of Power." *The American Political Science Review.* 56(4), 947–952. https://doi.org/10.2307/1952796 (accessed August 8, 2023)

42 Deshmukh, Pramod. Chairman Sanskriti Samvardhan Mandal Personal communication over email with Chloe Carroll and Maddy Horn April 23, 2018.

43 Meenakshi Nayar, ETASHA Society. Personal Interview over Zoom with Jason Mak April 21, 2018.

CORPORATE PROMISE AND REALITY

of impact and evidence-based interventions admit that not all valuable work is quantifiable.

For instance, advocacy campaigns to make legal changes or policy shifts can have enormous impacts but are almost impossible to measure in a quantifiable metric. Talking about the number of people who have seen a billboard doesn't tell us if the message on the billboard was effective. Often education about sanitation or advocacy to rewrite laws can take years and even decades before they result in a measurable impact on behavior. In fact, most of the deeper transformative work that involves remaking cultural norms or the distribution of resources and power in a community is slow work. It is often subterranean for long periods until a threshold is reached and then a cascading effect leads to changes that can remake whole communities. A corporate fixation on metrics and quantifiable results can lead to support for more superficial programs at the expense of more durable and transformative programs.

CSR Representatives & Companies

Looking at the backgrounds of CSR heads (who by law are required to also be on the executive board of the corporation), one can see three paths to the boardroom. In some cases, the CSR head is a family member of the CEO or owner of the corporation. This is most common in family-owned firms, which make up about 75% of businesses in India. Of these family corporations, over 100 are publicly traded companies.[44] When the corporation establishes its own foundation a member of the family, often a wife, is entrusted with the role of creating and executing a CSR policy.[45] The impersonal pathways to becoming CSR head are either to come to the position through the Human Resources department in the company or as someone from the CSO world who crosses over to join the corporate world. According to one CSO leader, "If the CSR head is from the development sector then we can work together but the ones where it's a HR person they don't get it." The orientation of CSR heads who have prior experience in HR is that they prioritize the needs of the company over those of the beneficiaries of social development projects. On the other hand, when a CSR head comes from the development sector,

---

44 Jayakumar, Tulsi. 2023. "India: State of Family Business Report" S.P. Jain Institute of Management and Research, Bharatiya Vidya Bhavan. Mumbai, India. Available at https://www.spjimr.org/wp-content/uploads/2023/09/cfbe-report-2023.pdf (accessed October 9, 2023)

45 Carroll, Aarti M. 2008. "India Inc's CEO wives head independent firms and trusts" *Economic Times* March 14.

they share a deep understanding and empathy with CSO workers. This allows "good things to happen."

As the CSR space matures, there may be a shift from novelty and experimentation to greater coordination and strategic planning. One example of this is that the public sector companies are working together to divide up all the districts of India so that CSR initiatives are spread more widely and don't just accrue to the most industrialized regions. They are increasingly partnering with research institutions like Ashoka University and Tata Institute of Social Sciences to identify priority issues and geographic areas. There are collaborations like those between Ashoka and the Haryana government which involve students in studying and implementing government schemes in coordination with CSOs. These are promising, but not yet fully developed models.

Impact

"Change and impact are not the same. Don't ask for impact in 2–3 years because that is too much to ask CSOs." This came from a CSR representative with Capgemini, a consulting corporation that pays attention to process. Instead, "you have to ask CSOs what their goals are, you can't dictate outcomes." This CSR head establishes goals over a 5-year period with their CSO partners, then breaks those down into quarterly targets so they can provide the accountability and impact assessment their executive board expects. How unusual this collaborative process is in most corporate–CSO partnerships was obvious to all the people attending this panel discussion. The moderator in fact laughed and said that now that the CSOs have heard about your process, "you will be mobbed after this panel." And it was true— the representative was surrounded by CSO workers pushing their brochures and visiting cards at him. Most CSR programs want impact assessments done regularly and the program to be wrapped up within a year. That is simply not a feasible time frame to achieve real change.

One CSR representative put it in stark terms, "If an NGO can't measure or quantify it, I will assume you haven't done it. Those days are gone where you can frame context. You have five minutes or 2 powerpoint slides to show what you have done, otherwise your chance is gone." While this may work for a program that is narrowly targeted, for example a vaccination drive, it cannot work for issues like increasing women's autonomy over their reproductive choices. A program that does that may not be able to assess its impact for a decade.

It should be noted, however, that there is one thing that large corporations are able to do—their size and their resources allow them to learn from failures

CORPORATE PROMISE AND REALITY 107

in a way that most shoestring budget CSOs cannot. "There are organizations that are working with different social enterprises lot of new models, use lots of new technologies so there is definitely things which are coming out from corporates again which have bigger budgets and they have that amount of leeway to have these, so when it fails they still have that we have tried it lets see what is the learning out of this. The bigger ones I would say want to do it but otherwise all midsize go with what's tried and tested," according to a longtime consultant. This willingness to experiment is a valuable practice and could benefit the social sector.

Mission Fit

The story above about ACC and their CSO partner is relevant to showing the challenges that come from a misfit between the goals of corporate partners and CSOs. Where the CSO workers wanted to engage in social work through sharing land and water management techniques with the mining-affected villagers, the company was interested in pacifying opposition to its work and improving its national reputation. As more and more workers realized that they were being used they attempted to speak up and represent the interests of the local community. They were told, "If you talk of ethics, our partnership will end here" by the company's CSR manager. "The local CSO leader was worried about the possible implications on the 'brand image' of Daan if it backed out from the CSR project, and the CSO losing 'credibility' among the corporate/business circles (whom he saw as future donors)."[46] The CSO leadership felt obligated to continue with the project in order to protect their future viability. The workers either quit or continued despite their reservations. And the company workers privately admitted that the goal of the projects was to support the continuation and expansion of mining operations. This CSR partnership was a performance that no one believed in.

Sonali's colleague at the child rights CSO explained that their organization also has to vet the companies they work with. "And then of course we need to make sure that that business is child-friendly, that they're not using child labor, there are certain parameter we set in place before we get into these corporate partnerships." Manufacturing firms have to certify their factories don't use child labor and companies that produce liquor or firearms are ruled out.

This CSO is large enough that they can conduct some due diligence in selecting corporate partners. But even here, there are limits to how

---

46 Kumar, U. 2018 "Mining, CSR, and the Politics of Attrition" University of Delhi.

intrusive and thorough their selection can be. Companies like Black Rock and CitiBank are partners of this CSO. Both are huge financial firms that prop up a global capitalist system that generates poverty and inequality. Their continued success arguably works at cross purposes to granting all Indian children an equal opportunity in life.

The corporate aversion to controversy also limits support for rights-based work. One consultant reports, "There are a lot of rights based organizations, you know the most traditional companies you will see won't fund these sort of organizations because, you know, things can change, things can move differently and all there is a lot of brand value attached to what they are doing. From a corporate's perspective it is not wrong—I mean for them the stakes are too high to be taking up something like this. If you still see [the] majority of the foreign funding is going into rights-based organizations and CSOs, not a lot of corporate funding goes to those. I think they would want to stay away from things like that. I think they would like to do something which they understand, this is the community I am working in, I see education is an issue, where access to health is difficult so this is something I understand and I will be able to bring in people and do. These rights-based approaches and everything of course have much longer gestation periods and requires lot of understanding while all the stakeholders, your committee and all want to see results as soon as possible which then of course happen in these sorts of projects which [are shallow]." This means that the kind of work that truly digs into social inequality is work that is not supported by CSR.

The Coca-Cola case that the chapter opens with also shows how the core business practice, the habits of consumption, the desires being cultivated are all in tension with the CSR goal of inclusive and sustainable development. Instead, CSR partnerships provide an alibi to corporations and cushion their reputations. The story of carpet company Interface, is a rare exception to the rule that company engagement with sustainability is surface and marketing related.[47] True transformation is possible, but rare.

Social Entrepreneurship

Social entrepreneurship is sometimes seen as an alternative to CSR–CSO incompatibility. It is supposed to combine the best practices of the corporate world with the heart and soul of the social work world.

---

47 Dean, Cornelia. 2007. "Ray Anderson: Executive on a Mission" *New York Times* https://www.nytimes.com/2007/05/22/science/earth/22ander.html (accessed May 6, 2022)

CORPORATE PROMISE AND REALITY 109

"Social entrepreneurship often exhibits some of the virtues commonly associated with commercial entrepreneurship, such as efficiency, dynamism, innovativeness, high performance, and economic sustainability."[48] This type of organization brings fresh eyes to the entrenched problems of inequality and poverty. Here there is no need to manage the different expectations of different organizations, rather the social entrepreneur itself melds the two. Is this the way to get around the history of mistrust and the ongoing tension in goals and methods evinced by corporates and CSOs? Below I describe a social entrepreneurship case study that shows that the hope for these organizations often outstrips their actual ability to transform the social landscape. It turns out that the problems they seek to solve are difficult for any organization, not just traditional nonprofits or the state.

Akshaya Patra is one of the most well-known social entrepreneurship organizations winning multiple awards and plaudits for its government–corporate–nonprofit collaboration. This Foundation is associated with the ISKCON religious organization, also known as the Hare Krishna movement.[49] The origin story of the foundation is that a temple in Bengaluru noticed that when they served a meal at the end of worship many children who were of school age would come to the temple to eat rather than attend class. The temple began to take food to neighboring schools thus reducing absenteeism and providing nutritious food to the children. From these organic origins, a Foundation was born that today provides about 1,800,000 meals per day as part of a Mid-day meal program in Indian schools.[50] Their website lists various awards and offers their virtues as transparency, leveraging partnerships, and efficiency in design and through technology.

The use of high efficiency central kitchens to cook the food and then distribute it to city schools brought widespread attention to Akshaya Patra Foundation.[51] Their centralized kitchens can purchase raw materials in bulk, deploy technology to cook at scale, and ensure quality control through monitoring procedures. This is in contrast to most mid-day meal provisions where the food is cooked in small batches at the school itself. The in-school method is much more labor intensive and not as efficient. Recently Akshaya Patra worked with Accenture Labs to apply blockchain,

---

48 Wei-Skillern, J., J. E. Austin, H. Leonard, and H. Stevenson. 2007. *Entrepreneurship in the Social Sector.* Los Angeles, CA: Sage Publications.

49 Religion Media Centre. 2022. "Factsheet: Iskcon" Available at https://religionmediacentre.org.uk/factsheets/iskcon-factsheet/ (accessed July 7, 2022).

50 Akshya Patra. 2022. "About Us" Available at https://www.akshayapatra.org/ (accessed July 7, 2022).

51 Keim, B. 2015. "Akshaya Patra" *Stanford Social Innovation Review* November 9.

110   CORPORATE SOCIAL RESPONSIBILITY AND CIVIL SOCIETY

artificial intelligence, and sensor-enabled devices to gather data and improve the efficiency of their central kitchens.

> An example of Akshaya Patra's transformation was its move from manual collection of feedback from children and schools to a more efficient technology-based solution. Using blockchain and sensor-enabled devices, the technical team gathered feedback digitally, leveraging AI technologies to predict the next day's meal requirements. The team tracked the timeliness of food delivered to each school involved in the initiative and collected the data using mobile devices and an Accenture-built system.[52]

The focus on efficiency and "disruptive technology" is unusual among CSOs and government service providers. Greater efficiency in their process allows Akshaya Patra to deliver more meals to more students at a lower cost.

Once Akshaya Patra moved into working in rural areas, its efficiency advantage was reduced as having a more dispersed population meant that centralized production didn't work as smoothly. In rural areas, the organization uses decentralized and hybrid kitchens which look much more like the programs run by state governments themselves. They hire a few women workers to cook the food at the schools themselves with some centralization of purchasing and a supervisor who moves from location to location to monitor the program.[53]

Critics have raised concerns about the sectarian underpinning of this organization in a religiously diverse country, its reliance on underpaid female workers, and financial improprieties caused by its rapid growth. The controversy over Akshaya Patra's religious foundation emerged with reports that the group refused to use onions and garlic in its meals.[54] Onions

---

52 Accenture. 2017. "Accenture Labs and Akshaya Patra" Available at https://newsroom. accenture.com/news/2017/accenture-labs-and-akshaya-patra-use-disruptive-technologies-to-enhance-efficiency-in-mid-day-meal-program-for-school-children (accessed May 14, 2024).

53 Rajaram, K and Brahambhatt, N. 2010. "The Akshaya Patra Foundation: Process Analysis" *UCLA Anderson School of Management* Case Study 11/2010. Available at https://www.anderson.ucla.edu/documents/areas/fac/dotm/bio/pdf_KRc.pdf (accessed July 13, 2022).

54 Nathan, A. 2019. "Why are Karnataka's school children unhappy with the mid-day meal?" *The Hindu* May 19. Available at https://www.thehindu.com/news/national/karnataka/why-are-karnatakas-schoolchildren-unhappy-with-the-mid-day-meal/article27378176.ece (accessed July 2, 2022).

CORPORATE PROMISE AND REALITY 111

and garlic are regarded as *tamsic* foods which increase negative, lustful energies according to Hindu scriptures. Soon after the organization also refused to include eggs in their meals despite campaigns by nutrition activists encouraging the inclusion of these high-protein foods in the program. Some states exempted the CSO from providing the eggs and found independent channels to distribute them.[55] Eggs are regarded as non-vegetarian by many upper-caste Hindus. The refusal to include eggs in the mid-day meals is a caste-based practice that many feel should not be subsidized by the state which is Akshaya Patra's largest funder.[56] Given the religious diversity of India's schools the adoption of a restricted diet that appeals to some upper caste Hindus is a highly contested practice.[57]

Akshaya Patra's efficiency also comes with a lower need for workers in its kitchens. By mechanizing a great deal of the cooking process, they are able to produce meals for 100,000 students with just 30 staff in one kitchen, 85,000 students with 80 staff in another.[58] In 2015, they had about 800 women workers in their centralized kitchens and 1400 in the decentralized kitchens. At that time, they had another 4500 or so male employees. By 2021, half their workforce was female as they expanded the number of decentralized kitchens where more cooking is being done by hand and in smaller batches.[59] As in many other industries, women are clustered in the lower-paying, less-mechanized arenas which also means their pay is lower than male colleagues. Across India, almost 2,500,000 workers are engaged in the production of mid-day meals. Most of them are women who are paid less than Rs 2000/month (about $24). According to a finance ministry official, this below minimum wage pay is explained, "The cooks and helpers are classified as honorary workers who have come forward to render social services. They are not considered workers and consequently, the legislations on minimum wages are not applied

---

55 Sharma, H. 2019. "MP Govt plans to add eggs" *India Today* October 31.

56 Jain, M. 2022. "Faith vs Nutrition" *Devex* February 26. Available at https://www.devex.com/news/faith-vs-nutrition-india-s-school-meals-program-walks-on-eggshells-102406 (accessed July 13, 2022).

57 For a defence of Akshaya Patra against secular Right to Food activists see: https://www.opindia.com/2018/12/foreign-funded-fcra-CSOs-behind-akshaya-patra-midday-meals-demand-to-remove-rafale-deal-complaint-demonisation-amarnath-yatra/ (accessed October 9, 2023)

58 Ahmad, S. 2018. "Akshaya Patra takes tech help" *Rediff* October 11. Available at https://www.rediff.com/business/special/akshaya-patra-takes-tech-help-to-better-feed-1761734-children-a-day/20181011.htm (accessed July 2, 2022).

59 Patra, Akshaya. 2021. "Celebrating superwomen" YouTube https://www.youtube.com/watch?v=HWBovHHACFA (accessed July 13. 2022).

to them."[60] The exploitation of these workers is worse in northern states than in southern states but is a problem across the board.

Finally, there have been high-profile board resignations from Akshaya Patra due to concerns about financial improprieties. Four of their board members resigned at the end of 2020 after having worked with the organization for about two decades. Former Infosys executives, Mohandas Pai and V Balakrishnan, Raj Kondur of ChrysCapital and Abhay Jain of Manipal Education and Medical Group resigned.[61] Soon after, civil society groups asked for a reassessment of the government's contracts with Akshya Patra due to their lack of transparency over how they manage funds and resources separately for the mid-day meal scheme and the larger temple trusts.[62] The petitioners said that according to Akshaya Patra, the cost per meal is Rs 6.03 of which the State government contributes Rs 4.14. Therefore, APF needs to raise Rs 1.89 in addition but despite requests, the Foundation was unwilling to provide details of how that money was raised and spent.

To conclude this case study, Akshaya Patra Foundation is widely considered a successful example of social entrepreneurship. The organization has brought innovation to the delivery of mid-day meals, in some cases doing it more efficiently than other groups or the state. Over time it has reduced its reliance on state funding and expanded its share of corporate and private donations. It adapted to school closures during the COVID lockdowns and stepped into a humanitarian role. The concerns about its proselytizing impulse as a religious organization shaping its service delivery, and the exploitation of field workers, especially women, are non-trivial. The fact remains that despite its growth and leveraging of economies of scale, Akshaya Patra only reaches about 3 million of the 118 million students who need a mid-day meal each day.[63] The state governments, local communities, and other CSOs carry much of the burden of meeting these needs.

---

60 Barman, S. 2021. "Most mid-day cooks paid less than 2000" *The Indian Express* December 21. Available at https://indianexpress.com/article/india/most-mid-day-meal-cooks-pay-7680906/ (accessed July 13, 2022).

61 *Times of India*. 2020. "Karnataka: Mohandas Pai, V Balakrishnan resign from Akshaya Patra Foundation" November 15. Available at http://timesofindia. indiatimes.com/articleshow/79228224.cms?utm_source=contentofinterest&utm_medium=text&utm_campaign=cppst (accessed October 12, 2023)

62 *The New Indian Express*. 2020. "Akshaya Patra fund misuse" November 25. Available at https://www.newindianexpress.com/states/karnataka/2020/nov/25/akshaya-patra-fund-misuse-now-civil-society-members-want-probe-2227734.html (accessed October 12, 2023)

63 BBC. 2022. "Mid-day meal plan struggles" April 22. Available at https://www. bbc.com/news/world-asia-india-61162642 and Akshaya Patra website. (accessed October 14, 2023)

Conclusion

In this chapter, the promise of corporate entry into the social development sector is scrutinized. By considering some of the key differences between CSOs and corporations, we can disaggregate the practices and goals of each type of organization. Then we can see how these potentially could be brought into creative dialogue so as to bring efficiency, transparency and a results orientation to a messy development sector. However, the reality is that these same qualities or desires can produce constraints that limit the effectiveness of aid interventions. Too short time horizons, a desire for easily quantified and measured results, and the emphasis on rigid reporting fail to produce the transparency, efficiency, and high-impact results everyone wants. Instead, they undermine the work of building trust with local communities, create incentives for shallow interventions rather than deeper transformative ones, and leave CSO workers frustrated. Based on the 55 largest firms, one study found that, "while firms that were initially spending less than 2% increased their CSR activity, those that were initially spending more than 2% *reduced* their CSR expenditures after Section 135 came into effect."[64] That is, in addition to the challenges of collaboration, the CSR law may have reduced the amount of money specific companies are spending on the social sector.

Looking at social entrepreneurs in particular, we can see the ways in which melding business practices with social goals can yield some exciting results. However, even here the results are difficult to scale and come with their own challenges and shortcomings. The reality of corporate social responsibility in India is that it is having a limited impact on sustainable and inclusive development.[65] Part of the lesson from this chapter should be that there is no one organizational form that can harness the best features of corporations and nonprofits and bring them into harmony. The fundamental divergence in mission drives too many other differences in these organizations. It is almost impossible to overcome this mission misfit. This is a main reason why it is so difficult to identify successful CSR partnerships.

> Since it's a government rule [Article 135] in a lot of areas we have seen the government comes in and demanding, 'look you have lot of CSR

---

64 Dharmapala, Dhammika and Vikramaditya Khanna. 2016. "The Impact of Mandated Corporate Social Responsibility: Evidence from India's Companies Act of 2013," CESifo Working Paper, No. 6200, Center for Economic Studies and ifo Institute (CESifo): Munich.

65 Mulky, Avinash. 2017. "Are CSR activities directed towards SDGs? A study in India" *OEFL Conference on Governance, Management and Entrepreneurship*, Dubrovnik: Croatia. https://repository.iimb.ac.in/handle/2074/12203 (accessed May 14, 2024)

114 CORPORATE SOCIAL RESPONSIBILITY AND CIVIL SOCIETY

money why don't you spend?', and a lot of things are under the prerogative of the government […] and they need to provide schools with these things specially under the RTE Act. There's so much that the government should be giving to these schools but nothing is there. A lot of times they use it as a substitute, that 'we have not done it and now you have this CSR money you do it', it's not. I mean it should fill in gaps which maybe, you know the government doesn't have expertise and government can't reach (because it's a big country) you can't reach all these places everywhere, but it should supplement what the government is doing, not take over the role which also happens.[66]

The danger that CSR can be seen as a substitute for the state is one that is deeply concerning. In a society where state accountability for quality social services is a huge challenge, if the state steps aside to invite corporate provision of services that will only harm the most oppressed.

---

66 Mulchandani, Payal. 2019. Personal Interview. Mumbai August 26.

Chapter 5

CIVIL SOCIETY RESPONSES

The influx of funds from corporate social responsibility (CSR) boards leaves civil society actors with three main responses: collaboration, rejection, and strategic partnership. This chapter centers the perspectives of civil society actors as they navigate the environment created over the past decade. As CSO actors describe their experiences trying to work with corporations, it becomes clear how frustrating these partnerships can be for them. They have to invest significant time and energy in building the partnerships even as the collaborations are too short and too output driven for meaningful social change. CSOs are of course a diverse range of actors. There are some that are extensions of political parties or those that are vanity projects. Despite the bad press that these CSOs get, most NGOs in the development sphere learn through practice what kinds of interventions are welcomed and which ones are not feasible on the ground. The description of the Sehgal Foundation's trajectory by its director is not atypical. "When we went to villages we thought we knew what they needed. After some time we discovered new needs and began working on those. We focus on a few villages and work on water, farming, education etcetera. Then neighboring villages see what we do and invite us to work with them." While the CSO came in with its own assumptions about what people needed, by staying in the field for a few years they built enough trust that they could learn what the community's own priorities were and they adjusted their programs to reflect those. This is what makes CSOs so critical to sustainable and inclusive development. They are offering services and goods that must be perceived as useful to their beneficiaries otherwise people will stop engaging with the CSO. This foundation now has over two dozen CSR and government partners who support its work.

In October 2019, an annual CSR Summit was held in New Delhi. The gathering brought together dozens of CSR professionals and hundreds of CSO workers. In the structure of the conference, the formal sessions, and the informal conversations over meals, I witnessed the challenges and opportunities created by the Companies Act. The exhibition section was staffed almost exclusively by either CSOs or consultants offering their services to

116   CORPORATE SOCIAL RESPONSIBILITY AND CIVIL SOCIETY

CSOs. Businesses were listed as sponsors of the conference in the welcome packets and hoardings placed around the hotel. This is where many of the CSO workers made their connections with others working in similar areas or tackling similar problems. In some cases, being in neighboring booths meant that they minded each other's space at the conference and developed plans to collaborate out in the real world too. Despite these collaborative possibilities, the truth was that most CSO exhibits were aimed at potential donors. And hardly any of these donors bothered to walk through the exhibition space. In part, this was because when they approached, they were quickly surrounded by eager CSO workers who thrust brochures and visiting cards at them. The possibility for informal networking among donors and CSO representatives was hard to come by. As one consultant described this kind of gathering, "most of these events have become a platform for, you know, where all the speakers are always from companies, some or the other PSU or corporate. This has become like all the NGOs are there, just take funds, talk to them and becomes like a very weird hierarchy process."

These formal panels constitute what James C. Scott refers to as the "public transcripts" of interaction between people with power over the less powerful.[1] This is the publicly authorized performance of their relationship in which the powerful tell a story that legitimizes their power. The less powerful group will go along with this performance—their compliance is an act of submission in itself. Public transcripts express the world according to the powerful, in our case according to corporate CSR representatives. They can be useful when understood in conjunction with "hidden transcripts" which are the ways in which the less powerful may respond to the powerful- by rolling their eyes, by enacting their roles poorly, or more rarely by openly contradicting the public transcript. In a situation of extreme exploitation, we would rarely have access to open dissent. In our situation of unequal but not oppressive relations, when CSO workers are in informal spaces or sometimes when they decide to push back against the version of the public transcript being offered by CSR donors, we can record their understanding of the relationship and its dynamics.

Public Transcripts

Along with a group of Lehigh undergraduate research assistants, I interviewed 15 CSOs in spring of 2019. Students were randomly assigned corporations

---

1 Scott, James C. 1992. *Domination and the Arts of Resistance*. New Haven, CT: Yale University Press.

CIVIL SOCIETY RESPONSES

(16) and CSOs from lists of large corporations and CSOs available online. We reached out to multiple organizations and conducted a combination of video calls, phone calls, and email exchanges. Some data were supplemented from the websites and annual reports of the organizations. Among the CSOs, seven had less than five corporate partners. In fact, five had no corporate partnerships. Three of them had more than 10 corporate sponsors for their work. Of those that did have corporate partners, these collaborations are quite recent and are likely prompted by the Companies Act provisions. Only one CSR–CSO partnership predated the passage of Article 135. All but four of the CSOs partner with the state in some way to deliver their programs or raise funds for them. About half of the CSOs working with corporations said they had changed as a result of the collaboration with mixed effects. The main shifts were in the accounting practices demanded by corporate donors. The other major impact was in the scale of the programs growing because of this new support. The law was seen as positive by both corporates and nonprofit social service organizations. A number of interviewees declined to respond to the question or were noncommittal which may indicate some hesitation about criticizing the law. We found support for the claim that NGOs can scale up their efforts in partnership. We also found some limited support that businesses will bring some of their more efficient and impact-oriented practices to the development sector. Beyond that, it appears that Article 135 was definitely having an impact in creating new partnerships by 2019. Many of these partnerships were still quite new and one struggle was to insure they become multiyear collaborations which can have a more transformative effect than short-term donations. The generally positive feelings about the CSR requirements suggest that the law was not creating an onerous burden on either the for-profit or nonprofit sectors as they adapt to it. Given the remote context and use of student interviewers, these results can be seen as a public transcript as CSOs reported on their corporate collaborations positively. Building rapport in person led to the discovery of other, more negative views of these partnerships.

In the formal sessions, the speakers were a mix of corporate representatives, senior government bureaucrats, the heads of major foundations, and CSO leaders. The framing of most of the talks, and the thrust of the Q&A was as advice to CSOs on how to learn enough about corporate desires to meet them. Panels on storytelling as a way to convey the theory of change and impact of a CSO, grant writing advice, and discussions of how to use technology to improve impact assessment were all about teaching CSOs how to package themselves for potential donors.

A few panels with donors explained what kinds of partners and projects they prefer to work with—innovative, scalable, and open to co-design. One

118   CORPORATE SOCIAL RESPONSIBILITY AND CIVIL SOCIETY

CSR board representative said, "Now we want to shift from philosophical to strategic CSR where CSR reflects our core competencies as a corporate." That is, they wanted to work with CSOs who are offering interventions that reflect the core competence of the business. In this case, the corporation was an information technology firm so they wanted to work with CSOs who have technological solutions to social problems. The question in the background of course is, what if the problem is not best addressed through IT? The representative went on to say, "We define our vision, then look at priorities. Lots of NGOs contact me, after all there is no dearth of causes. We have a 10 point selection criteria to identify credible partners. It's a matter of matchmaking." The relationships described here are as unequal as matchmaking in the Indian wedding market. Brides compete for grooms just as CSOs are competing for the attention of the CSR board. The speech came to its climax, "We are looking for trailblazers—those who have an x-factor that's attempting something new. Each of our partners is offering something innovative." The search for novelty may be exciting for the CSR representative but again, fails to account for the fact that many social problems don't require "innovative" or "trailblazing" projects. They require slow and deep connection and responsiveness to the people they are serving. There are few social problems that are resolved through quick technical fixes. Poverty and inequality persist precisely because of the way in which forms of inequality reinforce one another and the fact that some people gain from unequal social arrangements. To alter these social arrangements requires deep understanding of people, their relationships, and their trust as change begins. Much of the time that means that the CSO that has been in a community for a generation is much more effective than a new group that drops in with quick fixes.

Donors explained in a session on Digital Transformation that they need CSOs to provide data to their CSR representatives so they can take that to their board meetings when they ask for more support. An audience member, relying on a sign language translator, responded, "NGOs have limited organizational capacity. And we prioritize the mission over administrative processes. Companies should employ engineering graduates to create and analyze the data they require." This tension between the business needs of impact assessment and evaluation with the urgency of CSO mission work in lieu of capacity building is a recurrent tension. In another session, it was explained by a CSR representative that, "We ask our CSO partners to be digital and have an online presence. In a boardroom discussion people will look for you online so if there is no presence, [the] CSR head can't defend you. You should be honest online and have employee engagement possibilities." In this case, the CSR head is positioned as an advocate for CSOs who must make them legible to the rest of the corporate board. To educate and persuade them, the CSO must develop certain marketing strategies, among them, offering employee volunteering opportunities. For CSOs working with marginalized communities, the creation of volunteer experiences can be quite controversial, even harmful to the CSO's relationships with the community it serves.[2] In a panel about CSR and Education, it was observed that CSR leaders are, "pushing smart technologies and sideline teachers because they see teachers as a block to adopting new ideas." The promotion of technology at the expense of the people who make up the education system made working with CSR representatives a challenge for the CSOs who have to implement these programs.

Another masterclass on Strategic Marketing for NGOs offered research-based advice on how to communicate effectively. CSOs were encouraged to offer concrete and tangible examples rather than presenting broad data. "In storytelling the most important aspects are to highlight challenges and connections." Challenges can be shared through underdog stories where an unlikely individual overcomes great odds with the support of the CSO. And "connection plots" are stories that link the viewer/reader to the beneficiary. This advice was about how to market CSO work to CSR boards as well as individual donors. Increasingly, CSOs are becoming interested in retail fundraising and face the need to educate donors as well as the need to inspire potential donors to act on that education. Chetna Kaura explained how she convinced her company to pioneer a program to support transgender people. "As CSR head you have to educate your corporation to understand [the] development landscape, to educate them on impact and assessment. A focus on individual stories of impact help convey what the experience is like for one person." This also means letting go of ideas about scaling up a program as the chief measure of impact.

One of the most compelling speakers at the CEO Forum was Manasi Tata Kirloskar who is the fifth generation of the Kirloskar family to run their company. She said, "before we get into CSR we have to look at how business processes are actually happening. If you do business ethically within, then look out to the community. Business can be philanthropic in itself—see our factories employ people and they take care of their own families. We are shifting our plants to renewable energy sources and finding ways to recycle waste water. The CSR mandate was to push corporations to start thinking

---

2 Benevity. 2021. "Redefining Corporate Volunteering" *The Social Impact Show* August. Available at https://benevity.com/resources/redefining-corporate-volunteering (accessed November 2023).

about it if they weren't before." She offered a story about one of the CSR initiatives she had championed which sought to improve academic outcomes near one of her husband's factories (Tata factory). "CSR is about changing mindsets not giving paraphernalia. Building nice rooms, giving backpacks etc didn't help. Building toilets, especially girls' toilets didn't do it either. What worked was when we taught kids about the importance of sanitation and they pushed their families to build toilets in their homes." I came away from her speech struck by how she was so honest and willing to learn and do the hard work of working with others. Then I discovered that one of her family's firms had been involved in a major labor dispute in 2014 and management responded to the union's demands by locking the workers out—a hardball strategy designed to silence the workers.[3] Since then, her father and his brothers have been in a protracted legal battle over the legacy and funding of the business.[4] And the company was fined by India's Securities and Exchange Board for insider trading of shares.[5] How much of this Manasi knew about or was involved in is hard to say. But the talk of ethical business and management practices does not seem to be borne out by the public record.

Hidden Transcripts

The CSR summit included buffet lunch and tea breaks during which many of us took our plates to sit down at big banquet tables. I asked people about their work, what drew them to the conference, and what they were getting out of it. The people I spoke to do not represent a random sample of India's CSOs. The ones at this conference were already somewhat engaged with CSR and had sufficient organizational capacity to sponsor attendance at this summit. That means that the more established, wealthier, and more urban CSOs are over-represented in the voices heard here.

"Companies will never give money for real work—they care about profit," claimed one CSO leader who helps farmers grow sustainable cotton.

---

3 George, S. 2014. "Lockout at Toyota-Kirloskar: The Future Space for Labour." *Economic and Political Weekly*, 49(17), 18–20. http://www.jstor.org/stable/24480110 (accessed July 17, 2022).

4 John, Nevin. 2021. "Why Kirloskar Brothers Continue to Fight" *Fortune India* September 8. Available at https://www.fortuneindia.com/enterprise/why-kirloskar-brothers-continue-to-fight/105815 (accessed October 2023).

5 Upadhyay, J. 2020. "Sebi pulls up Kirloskar's promoters for fraud" *The Hindustan Times* August 12. Available at https://www.hindustantimes.com/business-news/sebi-pulls-up-kirloskar-s-promoters-for-fraud/story-yOc0er4IULaY8YGM9dIFhP.html (accessed October 2023).

She expressed her fear that corporations were only interested in educational interventions because they are easy to quantify and target children. She asks, "Who will farm? And how will our village kids compete with city kids?" These concerns are shared by many who see the push for homogenized education as a problem as much as it is a desirable solution to the marginalization of rural youth.[6] For those working on projects that support rural livelihoods without trying to connect them to the global economy there is very little support. "You have to do your research of the company. What are things they want or problems that need solving?" This environmental CSO head described the careful work that a CSO must do as they identify possible donors and approach them for a collaboration. Funding shapes programs and vision from both the corporate and nonprofit perspective.

Beyond this Summit, in interviews with CSOs at other times and places, I heard similar concerns raised by civil society workers. After asking the head of a small group that works with disabled people about his negligible dealings with corporations he shared his perception of the impact of Article 135 on smaller CSOs. "CSR people target only their benefit area from where they can earn more business. Secondly, big business houses have their own foundations or organizations of fixed NGOs they support. The real sufferers are the small NGOs working in rural or semi-rural areas, tribal areas like ours. Funding here by individuals, organizations, or CSR is very, very low."[7] One reason that smaller CSOs rarely partner with corporations is that they don't have the capacity to meet the accounting and impact assessment requirements of CSR boards. Below, I organize comments from CSO representatives based on whether they are in enthusiastic partnerships with corporations, purposely reject working with corporations, or are strategically engaged with them.

Collaborators: Talking about funding, one CSO worker pointed out that, "CSR funding is hard to get. We have to help CSR people learn about the sector so they don't cause problems or waste money. I hear that corporations have demands, but we need to go beyond that." This CSO worker is articulating the desirability of CSR funds for their work and acknowledging that to get the money they have to either jump through hoops that don't make sense or they have to invest time and effort into educating their CSR partners about their work. That means that beyond the formal work of grant writing and meeting to align priorities and budgets, CSOs who partner with corporations are also engaged in a delicate process of teaching their donors about the social

---

6 Jain, Manish. 2018. "Our work is to recover wisdom and imagination" Podcast episode January 31. Available at https://www.robhopkins.net/2018/01/31/manish-jain-our-work-is-to-recover-wisdom-and-imagination/ (accessed November 2021).

7 Personal interview over Zoom, April 2018.

problems they want to tackle. "They call us to their fancy offices and say explain your work in 30 minutes. And from January–March their calls become urgent as they have to close their books then." Even as CSR offices know they require education about the social sector and invite partners, they want that education on their terms and timelines. This structures the relationship as one of patron and beneficiary between the company and the CSO, rather than the partnership they claim to seek.

One feminist CSO leader described the transition from seeking funding from foreign aid agencies to corporations by saying, "There are only 4–5 corporates who are good and it's a matter of finding them. The bilaterals will fund an idea and the proposal may evolve as the information comes in. With a corporate, they define impact first and work backwards from that and want a tangible result." When I pressed her to explain why that was a problem, she explained "Social sector needs time. We suggested a continuum of care approach from a 10 year old girl to her marriage age of around 21 years and they told us '*tum paagal ho*' [you are crazy]. They can't do something holistic and long term. They fund for only 1 or 2 years." Where international organizations and bilateral aid agencies were never regarded as ideal donors, in comparison to corporations they are seen as more flexible and more willing to wait for social change to unfold gradually. The corporations are seen as both overly concerned with outputs—those tangible results that can be measured, and as impatient.

Another CSO leader told me that one corporation asked for a partnership that would end anemia in all the villages in their area. "They just don't know the field reality. Experimentation is needed, but it's not based on research at all." The leader liked the goal of ending anemia but knew that this would take more than a year's work as the underlying causes of anemia are linked to lack of information about *and* access to high iron foods and because of sexist norms that leave women with inadequate nutrition and sanitation, while also encouraging early marriage and childbearing. Shifting the social norms will take much longer than simply providing iron supplements to all girls and women, but equal status for women is required to actually end chronic anemia. Along the same lines, another education related CSO said that, "Most collaborations are one sided with businesses, average business tries to take an upper hand." He said that having worked with CSR boards had impacted his CSO in some positive ways. "We report better, communicate better and probably track better. Overall we have become more professional."[8] What had changed for the CSO was that it was getting better at making

---

8 Personal interview over Zoom. April 9, 2019.

its operations legible to funders. Another group that serves the disabled community, explained its CSR partnerships as fairly transactional. "Since most of the companies had a lot of experience and knowledge on marketing, most companies provided us funds and handled the marketing side of the partnership."

At the CSR Summit, one corporate sector representative explained that building partnerships takes effort. Speaking of the liminal role played by the CSR board in a corporation's executive board, a CSR representative explained, "We were all part of the NGO sector at one point so we can go beyond corporate demands to figure out how to collaborate. People have to hit it off, they must gel with partners, then the project assumes a life of its own." He is speaking to the way in which many CSO workers have crossed over to join the corporate sector as CSR representatives. They bring with them deep empathy for the CSO workers and they understand that the best recipe for a successful intervention are the people and relationships involved. Social problems require sociality. I return to this later in the chapter.

One CSO my research assistant spoke with described an unusual situation, Child Rights and You (CRY). They do collaborate with corporations but are able to do so on their own terms as corporate funding "is a small piece of a bigger pie. So now we have a whole bunch of privileged people, mainly the middle class from who we get very small amounts to very big amounts." They mostly rely on small donors to fund their programs and corporate funding is a supplement to that. "I think CRY is one of the very few organizations in India that has received overwhelming support from corporates. Because now there is so much red tape when dealing with corporates and you know the bigger the corporate, the more the bureaucracy and that kind of stuff. But somehow, CRY's message gets through and we have had several corporates from all across India, small corporates and big corporates, support our cause." She explains that the focus on children and their ability to navigate the bureaucratic needs of corporations make them a favored CSO.[9] The founder of a skill training CSO told us, "As an organization we have right from the start, we have either worked with individual donations or corporate funding. And we found that with the kind of work we were doing and we were very number driven so we attracted a lot of corporate support, companies who were into supporting society even before [Article 135] came to be."[10] She emphasized that the type of work and

---

9 Representatives for CRY. Personal Interview on Skype. April 25, 2018.
10 Personal interview over Skype. April 21, 2018.

impact assessment this CSO was able to do made them legible to corporations and that attracted them to collaborate.

In another interview, we asked someone from a road safety organization how CSR collaboration was different from other types of donor relations. "Yeah, with the corporations the clients are very different especially in terms of what they want which has to be factored in accordingly. Many corporations are very interested in getting their organization visibility by doing CSRs and you don't see that with individual [donors]. A conversation with a corporate have to change depending on what their needs are, their needs might be branding, their needs might be employee engagement, so on and so on. And whatever the case may be—so long as it doesn't compromise the project—we will try to include those things because those are the things corporations look for."[11] He was clear that corporations have a different relationship with CSOs than other types of donors. They are both more bureaucratic and more capricious with what they want. And since they have so much more money to offer, they can generally get what they want. Another CSO leader of a Hindutva group, was quite happy about working with corporations but agreed that they are different from other types of donors. "The business work more professionally, more paperwork like documentation, accounting etc. Individual donors are more versatile and liberal to modify, revise their projects as and when it is necessary." Overall he was very enthusiastic about the CSR law and the steps taken by the Modi government to root out "on paper only NGOs." But even he noted that corporate collaborations required more adherence to preset plans and less flexibility in response to ground realities.

Rejection: In the course of this research, I also spoke with many CSO actors who refuse to work with corporations. They may collaborate with bilateral agencies, or even the foundations associated with corporations, but they don't work with the corporate board itself. In addition to these refuseniks, there are also CSOs that specifically challenge and resist neoliberalism and capitalism. One feminist CSO leader explained, "What we are seeing is the state shrinking its own role and therefore it's shirking accountability. In this neoliberal context our human rights work is not compatible with CSR."[12] The rejection of (or absence of) corporate funding is most common among advocacy based CSOs. Later in that discussion, scholar of Indian philanthropy, Pushpa Sundar, explained that generally advocacy oriented CSOs, like those concerned with human rights, are the least likely to take

---

11 Personal interview over Skype. April 26, 2018.
12 Personal interviews. New Delhi. July 2019.

CSR funding. This is because their work is seen as politically controversial and knowing that they are unlikely to be funded, the CSOs make a virtue out of necessity and claim they are rejecting corporate sponsors. Another major scholar and rights-based activist, Reetika Khera, agreed with Sundar. "Many people in civil society are also just doing a *naukri* (job). Social movements think they are superior because they are not funded [by corporations or foreign agencies] but they themselves lack internal democracy and end up mooching off funded NGOs in their network." She suggests that taking corporate funding directly or not is meaningless. What the CSO or social movement activist actually does with its resources is more significant.

One of the organizations that doesn't have any corporate partners, explains why they have not created any CSR partnerships. "The problem with CSR is that the companies have leverage to decide who they want to support. They want their money to go to areas that are conducive to them. They often prefer to work in the areas of child and women because those are the areas that garner the most attention. Education also is another area where businesses prefer to enter. Being an NGO working with depression and distress, it is not a topic which many companies want to associate their brand." When pressed about CSR collaborations that could have been, he told us, "We have had offers from companies pertaining to CSR especially from pharma[ceutical] companies, but the pharma companies comes with their own agenda. They want and expect us to be able to raise the company's prominence. But we are what we are and cannot accept that type of relationship where there is an accountability we are unable and not interested in undertaking. We don't want anyone else to decide what we should be doing and how we are doing it just because they are paying for it."[13] This director's commitment to the privacy of the people he served and desire to have operational autonomy led him to reject overtures from CSR representatives.[14] This was confirmed by another children's CSO whose representative said the CSR law had brought a lot of money into the nonprofit field, "but I do not know where truly that money goes to because we aren't able to get any funding. I do not venture out into a field simply because of the funds. I want the funds to come to where I am. CSR is good but only caters to large NGOs in big cities which is unfair."[15] The partnerships depend on both a fit between missions and also ease of access for the corporations. Given the regional

---

13 Personal interview over Skype. April 26, 2018.
14 Personal interview. April 25, 2018.
15 Personal interview over Zoom. Tamil Nadu. April 12, 2019.

inequality in India, it means that most of the CSR support is provided in areas that are relatively well off already.[16]

Another organization that is entirely volunteer based explained, "We do not accept funds directly. But a lot of corporates have made donations in time. Like we do not accept any money, but they sometimes they buy rations for us. We do not raise funds from corporations, we do not want funds from the government, or from the public." This CSO tries to meet local needs as they are defined by deprived communities through volunteer work and episodic service provision. They believe there is less room for things to go wrong if no money is involved even if it limits the scale of their operations. Transparency and confidence are words that came up a lot. When asked how CSR partners are distinctive, he said, "so when we are working with businesses, a lot of times there a lot of legal requirements that need to be done. A lot of paperwork." This group has a mutual aid model of operation that rejects the corporate CSO model altogether.[17] They believe the intrinsic rewards of ordinary people helping each other is the best way to create solidarity and trust.

Strategic partners: Asked about their partnerships, a girl's rights CSO told us, "[…] it is a strange relationship. The corporate holds the money and the power and can be quite demanding of what they want. For example, one of our sponsors for the slum school for 3 years and we just meet with them, and they were being very specific of what they want. They only want to focus on education, but we work in the slum. We also do health prevention work; we work with women […]. They were very specific that they would only pay for the education of children. We are not going to change the service we offer, but they were only going to fund certain programs. Then we have to go find another funder."[18] This is a classic example of a CSO understanding that to achieve their goals—no violence against women and children—they have to support the whole family through education, health care, empowerment, and capacity building. But the corporation only wants to support the least controversial and most easily quantified service—number of children in a school. In fact, we spoke to one of their corporate partners and they explained that for each project they take on they like to have a clear goal such as, "we try to get 500 students who have never been to a school we are

---

16 Rossow, R. M. 2015. "Corporate Social Responsibility in India: How the companies act may augment regional disparities" Center for Strategic and International Studies, Washington DC.

17 Spade, Dean. 2020. *Mutual Aid: Building Solidarity during This Crisis (and the next)*. London, UK: Verso.

18 Personal interview over Skype. Pune. April 12, 2019.

trying to enroll them" and that "I personally and my team members are very hands on. We visit them [the CSO run school] and keep engaging with them in case something goes wrong."[19] He admitted that the corporation had only been providing this CSR support for a year. Despite that, he felt comfortable telling the CSO what to do and how to measure success.

Strategic partners is the category that most CSOs find themselves in—one in which they identify specific donors who will support ongoing programs or have multiple donors—a kind of diversified portfolio. In fact, one CSR representative complained, "Don't look at corporations as a bank, I'm looking to co-create something with you [CSOs]. You are not flexible, you already have a program and just want funding." This dynamic is one that corporations dislike but is actually the preferred mode for most CSOs. They would like to develop their work in response to grassroots needs and then find sponsors to support that work. However, this strategy is usually not successful at capturing CSR funding. One consultant told me, "I think even if organizations—NGOs are suggesting to do different things which might be more of a priority in that area than say education or health, people, companies had to go with those because they understand more, for them to show them in a report or for them to show anyone in just a simpler thing you know and everyone wants to work with kids, everyone wants to work on health, because you want to go with what is easily understood to all the stakeholders." The companies do not want to support the priorities identified by the grassroots CSO. Instead they prioritize what will make sense to the corporate board. Some corporations have begun to pool their CSR expertise and funding. "Corporations do collaborate with one another. We struggled initially because of egos and logos but now we have found ways to work together." A number of CSR representatives spoke optimistically about the government's work identifying "aspirational districts" in which needs were identified and different companies (mostly public sector enterprises) were asked to support the people in those districts. "The main impediment to development is the multiplicity of schemes and lack of convergence. The aspirational district program is trying to overcome this thanks to Niti Ayog." According to MP Sujeet Kumar, the state of Odisha is a leader in coordinating CSR. They identified its nine most deprived districts and decreed that 59% of CSR spending must take place there along with an equivalent proportion of government social spending. Initiatives like this are promising in that they are need based rather than proximity based. However,

---

19 Personal interview over Skype. April 20, 2019.

128   CORPORATE SOCIAL RESPONSIBILITY AND CIVIL SOCIETY

they still do not demonstrate sensitivity to the social and historical patterns that lead to deprivation.

A literacy promotion CSO founder told us that the passage of the CSR law had doubled or even tripled the financial support they were receiving for their work. Again, their projects are easy to quantify and measure. "I would like to say is, so far the CSR has come to stay and the CSR is enhancing the partnership between the NGOs and the corporates. But there is also a give and take, a mutual learning that has to happen." He gave the example of corporations only wanting to support projects close to their own operations even if 300 km away the need is much greater. "So, the corporates should learn to move from their immediate areas to the needy areas. In a similar way, NGOs should also learn the professional way of working with the corporates in terms of giving proper indicators, giving proper outcomes and outputs so that we are able to relate what we are doing and generate proper reports to the corporates."[20] Even as he endorses the shifts in CSO operations, he is revealing how significant the changes are in the day-to-day operation of civil society. The leader of a water and sanitation CSO described the challenges in collaborating with corporations because his CSO primarily focuses on the software- building capacity and training people, rather than hardware—building toilets and water treatment plants. Corporations "would come in very strict minded, focused on hardware delivery, service delivery and restricted geographies of their choice. And it will be hard for us to match those." But by persevering and educating the companies, they have been able to overcome some of this to the point that corporations will fund their work. The corporations still want to avoid anything advocacy-related, and they have introduced much more paperwork. "Now you have different donors, some asking for our annual templates and coming back because they are happy with the work we are doing [...] Some of our other donors would want to sit every day and kind of manage those programs on an everyday basis with a lot of new templates, which means a lot of transaction costs. Which also means that we have to actually put in special servicing units to serve these specific donors rather than use through our one or two single templates for all."[21] Unlike previous institutional donors which accepted the CSO's reporting template or individual donors who mostly don't ask for budget statements, the corporations need to report on spending to their CSR boards. Their deep pockets let them dictate the forms, the templates, that must be used. And so the CSO that wants to work with them must

---

20 Personal interview on Skype. January 2018.
21 Personal interview on Skype. April 20, 2018.

CIVIL SOCIETY RESPONSES

develop the institutional capacity to provide the data in the format requested. As anyone who has applied for a grant knows, the forms you must fill out shape the story you tell about your work, they shape the process, and they shape future directions you move into.

Rise of the Consultants

The massive expansion of CSR in the past decade has led to the creation of a new sector of consultants. These groups connect corporations with CSOs, conduct participatory assessment studies of needs in neighborhoods, help design interventions, implement projects, and rigorously measure impact. These consultants often hire their workers from CSOs and are a combination of development professionals and corporate refugees who are seeking more meaningful work. Bridgespan group was founded in 2015, 4th Wheel Social Impact also started in 2015, Sattva Consulting began in 2009, Samhita began working in 2010, and so on. In addition to their role-facilitating partnerships, the consultants conduct sectoral research and hold gatherings, including award ceremonies for CSR and CSO professionals. "CSRBox, Dasra, Ardhan, GiveIndia, Milaap, Keto, Global Giving- all online consultancies exist because the system is not streamlined or clear." One CSO head explained that they had to create profiles and submit their information to multiple websites that claim to vet nonprofits and make them easy to find for potential donors. The government created its own NGO portal but, "Even Darpan was a good idea but its not updated so it becomes useless." explained the CSO activist.[22]

Online presence is essential for CSOs that want to be in the CSR game. The consultancies often began as communications specialists, helping CSOs craft a brand and communicate it to potential partners and donors. "If they are looking for a nonprofit that matches their policy, they typically turn to online sources to locate the organizations that are working in that space and sometimes they also hire consultants which are a real boon, that is typically, I think because of the CSR law. CSR consultants have kind of mushroomed across the space, basically because the organizations have a lot of funds but they don't know much about how to invest it in the development sector, these intermediary organizations have grown up. They help them with how to make a CSR policy, how to monitor the nonprofit, they've even developed online formats and all that. Nonprofits can put in their data like for GiveIndia [...]. The main shift is that across many nonprofits over the last

---

22 Personal interview. New Delhi. July 2019.

130   CORPORATE SOCIAL RESPONSIBILITY AND CIVIL SOCIETY

2–3 years you'll see a shift of funds coming from corporations which would typically have been a small percentage now being a much larger percentage. It would have grown to several times, so if it was 2% now it might be 40% because that is the amount of money that is now coming in."[23]

The fact that most of the CSOs collaborating with corporations described how those partnerships led them to alter their internal processes is noteworthy. For instance, a skill training organization reports, "Changes in our activities includes [sic] increased compliance and financial monitoring capacity. Training and capacity building of Finance and Operations teams internally to meet reporting requirements."[24] They have adapted to the reporting requirements of their corporate partners. Initially building capacity was often done with the support of consultants who taught nonprofits how to think about their processes like businesses do. But over time, organizations internalized this jargon and methodology.

Dasra was the original organization that provided research and professional support to CSOs and donors in India. Their work began in 1999. According to co-founder Nundy, "Because of the exposure we had, whether it was Morgan Stanley or working with nonprofits, we realised that there was a role we could play to bridge the distance between where funding is (educating donors to be more strategic in their giving) and the NGOs so that they could use those funds in the most optimum manner. So, we like to call ourselves an NGO for NGOs because that's really where a lot of our motivation comes from."[25] Meera Nundy and her partner Deval Sanghavi came to this role via the corporate sector, lending their business process lens to the goals of CSOs. The organization has been highly successful in speaking to corporate and high net worth donors, educating them about how to direct their giving. Their familiarity and access to these donors have also made them highly sought after by CSOs who want to adapt to donor desires. Dasra supplies education for donors, capacity building for CSOs and coordinates networks who want to achieve specific goals over three- to five-year periods.[26] Over the past two decades, Dasra has grown rapidly and continues to be one of the most important bridge builders between the corporate and nonprofit worlds.

Many CSOs acknowledge that access to CSR funding takes some kind of personal connection. For those with board members who come from

---

23 Personal Interview on Skype. April 26, 2018.
24 Email correspondence. March 26, 2019.
25 Dastur, Tina. 2017. "The Do-Gooders" The Verve Available at https://www. vervemagazine.in/people/the-do-gooders-neera-nundy-and-deval-sanghavi (accessed October 2023; site inactive by July 2024).
26 Dasra. 2023. "About Us" www.dasra.org (accessed October 2023).

the corporate world, the introduction to CSR boards is smooth.[27] But for those who do not have corporate representatives on their nonprofit boards, it is much more challenging to be seen as a credible and reliable partner. In fact, some have warned that the presence of so many wealthy trustees can pose a danger to CSOs. Oxfam India's Director Amitabh Behar argues that as CSOs adopt corporate management techniques, they orient toward decontextualized impact instead of "bottom-up, people-led processes built around trust." They also lower the level of risks the organizations are willing to take, avoiding conflict even when some is appropriate and lead to a disconnect with local communities.[28] The processes described here are the flip side of the transfer of people from the social sector to the corporate and consulting world.

This transfer of people and processes from the corporate world to the nonprofit world and vice versa needs more attention. Can we think of the movement of CSO workers from civil society to CSR boards and foundations as a kind of "brain drain" where the social sector is losing talented people to higher salaries? If that is the case, there is a kind of self-fulfilling prophecy at work. Initially, corporations saw civil society as lacking imagination and innovation in solving the challenges of inclusive and sustainable development. If enough talented people leave the sector to join a consulting group or a CSR unit within a corporation. This is one aspect of the "corporatization of civil society." As ambitious and experienced professionals move from the civil society sector to the corporate sector, there are compromises that are made. The idea of "golden handcuffs" is that the bigger paychecks and better benefits that come with working for a large corporation or foundation can make it harder for the idealistic social change worker to actually effect the transformations in society they seek.[29] In order to fit in with the culture of the new organization, in order to preserve the salary and benefits their families are counting on, CSO workers who have become CSR representatives soften their critiques and become team players. It's just they now play for the corporate team.

---

27 Personal Interview on Skype. April 28, 2018.
28 Behar, Amitabh. 2020. "The changing nature of nonprofit boards" *Times of India* August 31.
29 Arenas, Andrea. 2023. "Philanthropy's golden handcuffs" *Community Centric Fundraising* August 7. Available at https://communitycentricfundraising.org/2023/08/07/philanthropys-golden-handcuffs-the-illusion-of-liberation-and-the-complex-balance-between-self-preservation-and-complacency-among-foundation-workers/ (accessed December 2023).

Responding to Corporate Collaboration

This chapter has shown that when it comes to civil society–corporate collaborations, two fairly distinct public and hidden transcripts are available. In the public transcript, civil society is timid and fusty, afraid to take risks or try new approaches. The corporations arrive as partners who provide funds but also the backbone to encourage innovation and disruption in the social sector. In the hidden transcripts, civil society workers describe having to do a lot of work to educate the corporate representatives on the nature of social work. They describe an unequal dynamic in which corporations use their superior funds to try and direct what the CSO does in its programming. All CSOs also claimed that they find ways to resist this pressure either by being highly strategic about their collaborations or by refusing them altogether. Even the ones who think they are able to negotiate collaboration in a way that keeps their mission intact usually adapt their work to include the kinds of accounting, reporting, and assessment that corporations seek.

The investment in institutional capacity required to meet reporting requirements inevitably shapes the kind of work a CSO actually does. In the same ways that foreign aid can distort the agendas and perspectives of CSOs, corporate funding can encourage a focus on particular types of problems and the identification of certain solutions over others. It also discourages CSOs from full frontal attacks on capitalism or the growing power of corporations. After all, any CSO that is receiving or may one day hope to receive corporate funding can hardly be seen as an enemy of capitalist economic development. This is a considerable narrowing of the field of vision for CSOs in the development sector. "Funding has fragmented solidarity in ways that repression never could."[30] Socialist, Gandhian, anarchist, communist, indigenous, and other alternatives to a market economy cannot be embraced by CSOs that are part of the collaborative ecosystem. In the absence of a civil society voice examining these options and reminding society that the market economy is not a natural or necessary fiction, the market-based path can feel inevitable. The loss of imagination involved is a grave threat to inclusive democracy and environmental sustainability and ultimately amounts to the ideological corporatization of civil society.

---

30 Roy, Arundhati. 2014. *Capitalism: A Ghost Story* Chicago, IL: Haymarket Books.

Chapter 6

AFTER CORPORATE SOCIAL RESPONSIBILITY

How can we assess the effects of mandatory corporate social responsibility (CSR) in India? There are a variety of impacts and measures that we can attend to. Among these, the most immediate is the expansion of funds flowing from corporations to the social sector. The number of firms engaged in CSR increased in the years after 2013, especially among those engaged in consumer-oriented business.[1] Before the passage of Article 135 making CSR mandatory, Indian CSR spending was estimated at $403,651,039.[2] Four years later, in 2017, CSR spending was about $2,050,255,332, and five years later, in 2022, it was around $3,109,548,883, an increase of about a billion USD.[3] This growth from about $400 million to $3.1 billion over a decade is astonishing. Should this increase in spending be seen as a success? This book offers reasons to think that more CSR should not be seen as a good thing.

As described in the introductory chapter to this book, the Nihilists warned that CSR can displace the role of the state in providing social services, undermine democratic accountability by falsely depoliticizing development decision-making, and whitewash corporate harms, which allows corporations to become even more wealthy and powerful. In India, despite many CSOs pursuing emancipatory politics, the existence of Hindutva xenophobic organizations, and apolitical corporate-led CSOs, creates a complex picture

---

1 Dharmapala, Dhammika and Vikramaditya Khanna. 2016. "The Impact of Mandated Corporate Social Responsibility: Evidence from India's Companies Act of 2013," CESifo Working Paper, No. 6200, Center for Economic Studies and Ifo Institute (CESifo), Munich.

2 Bansal, Sangeeta and Shachi Rai. 2014. "An Analysis of CSR Expenditure in India." *Economic and Political Weekly* 49, 50.

3 CSR Portal. 2023. "CSR Expenditure: Summary," Government of India. Available at https://www.csr.gov.in/content/csr/global/master/home/home.html (accessed November 2023).

of civil society. In the 1990s, as the role of the state moved away from public goods provision, "it opened up policymaking to non-state actors. [...] However, as policy networks emerged, the dominant non-state actors tended to be and have been businesses and their āssocations, or international global influences. [...] Civil society's participation remained limited to issue-based inputs on an adhoc basis." Hindutva CSOs and the corporate ones are aligned with the state in reducing democratic space for dissent while the secular CSOs are being prevented from playing their role as guarantors of democracy.[4] The growth of CSR is a problem as it is part of the matrix reducing democratic space for dissent.

To be clear, nothing in my interviews with dozens of CSOs or corporations suggested that the people involved had malevolent intentions. Everyone agreed that India has a problem in that the phenomenal growth of the past two decades hasn't trickled down sufficiently. They all wanted to find ways to support more inclusive and sustainable development. In this sense, the Nihilists are too critical in that they ascribe malign motives to corporate representatives, and actually, the truth is sadder than they recognize. Corporate representatives truly can't see any alternatives to the development path we are on. Therefore, they think the best hope is for corporations to share their vision and tools with the rest of society. They either can't see or can't articulate any other possibility beyond market capitalism.

The language of civil society has long been a technomoral language in which claims are made using ethical visions of the public good.[5] Within the negotiations between corporations, the state, and civil society, CSR blurs boundaries and undermines the legitimacy of civil society claims by allowing companies to also position themselves as champions of the marginalized. The growth of CSR and billionaire philanthropy reduces civil society's ability to offer alternative narratives. "Dissent is the most important role of civil society since the colonial period. Not all collaboration is partnership," warns Pushpa Sundar.[6] She sees the space for civil society to dissent from the governing ideology of the state and large corporations being undermined through CSR and state-funded collaborations once "[...] the NGO sector itself began to look increasingly to the corporate sector for

---

4 Singh, Richa and Amitabh Behar. 2018 "India Civil Society: Beyond the Cooperation-Competition Binary," in Raffaele Marchetti (Ed.). *Government-NGO Relations in Africa, Asia, Europe and MENA*. Routledge: London.

5 Bornstein, Erica and Aradhana Sharma. 2016. "The Righteous and the Rightful: The Technomoral Politics of NGOs, Social Movements, and the State in India." *American Ethnologist* 43, 76–90.

6 Personal interview. New Delhi. July 2019.

AFTER CORPORATE SOCIAL RESPONSIBILITY 135

financial support as it experienced a shortage in foreign aid that was governed by geopolitical considerations and trends in funding. This compromised the NGO sector's autonomy because of increasing financial dependence on the corporate sector."[7] The financial links between civil society and corporations reduce the watchdog role of CSOs and undermine corporate accountability. A funded collaboration is very rarely a true partnership unless the actors involved take explicit steps to manage their unequal power relations.[8] So far, CSR collaborations don't demonstrate this level of self-awareness.

Corporatization of Civil Society

The culture clash between corporations and civil society rests on fundamental differences between their organizational type. They are structured and oriented to value different goals, and therefore they employ divergent strategies and processes. As a reminder, some of these key differences are discussed in Chapter 1. Both corporations and CSOs are intermediary institutions that connect individuals to others beyond the family for a variety of end goals. While corporations create and market goods and services, CSOs create and market a vision and services. In the corporate world, people are viewed as *homo economicus*, autonomous, and able to engage in voluntary exchanges based on their individually formed preferences. People maximize their self-interest, and the goal of the organization is to make a profit. In the CSO world, humans are deeply embedded within social relations with identities and obligations that stem from these relationships. Each person can pursue their own definition of a good life in ways that are completely unrecognizable to another. In the corporate world, growth and self-interest are guiding principles, while in the CSO world, meaning and relationships are guiding principles. These differences lead each of these sectors to regard the other as a danger and threat to itself.

When pressed into a partnership because the corporation is the one with the money, the CSO has to adapt itself to the processes demanded by the corporation. This is not just a transaction cost. It also subtly shapes the agenda and methods used by the CSO in carrying out its work. The demand for quantifiable impact assessment, the demand for marketing material, and

---

7 Sood, Atul and Bimal Arora. 2006. "The Political Economy of CSR in India." UNRISD Publications: Issue 18.

8 Rajeshwari, B., Nandini Deo, and Margit van Wessel. 2023. "A Feminist Approach to Collaboration: A Sex Worker's Network in India," in Bawole, J., Kontinen, T., and van Wessel, M. (Eds). *Reimagining Civil Society Collaborations: Starting from the South*. London: Routledge.

136 CORPORATE SOCIAL RESPONSIBILITY AND CIVIL SOCIETY

the need to limit projects to 1–3-year cycles are all part of the corporatization of civil society. It encourages CSOs to narrow their ambitions and perspectives so that they can set clear targets and meet them. After all, if your goal is to get 5,000 students to attend a workshop, that is easy to measure. If your goal is to build a feminist consciousness among youth, that is a bit more complicated. If your aim is to achieve gender equality through education and mentoring networks, you are looking at a goal that will take at least a decade or two to achieve. If you want to work with corporations, it would be much wiser to adopt the quantifiable and short-term service delivery goals. This is a corporatization of civil society agendas.

The increasing regulations imposed by the government combined with the demands of corporate partners for budget and accounting transparency also are part of the corporatization of civil society organizations.[9] Creating Excel sheets and tracking interactions, as well as translating relationships into the language of service delivery, brings the impersonal efficiency of a corporation into the complex and messy world of nonprofits. The greater legibility of what the CSO does leads to greater value being placed on what can be made legible and devalues the emotional work that underwrites many development interventions.[10] In this way, the corporatization of civil society operations influences their agendas and perspectives.

The loss of imagination involved in the self-censoring of civil society organizations is the greatest loss taking place. It can be described as the ideological corporatization of civil society. This is a state in which CSOs narrow their vision to operate within the existing market capitalist system. It happens when they accept that inequality, exploitation of natural resources, and endless growth are the only options for economic and social development. Inclusive and sustainable development are treated as the product of business-led growth and minor redistribution by the state and civil society. This is the ideological corporatization of civil society and is a danger to the future of our world. If we can't imagine alternative futures, we can't create them.

The revolving door of professionals moving from the social sector into consulting roles or onto CSR boards and the adoption of corporate leaders

---

9 Srinath, Ingrid. 2022. "Covid-19, Corporatisation and Closing Space: The Triple Threat to Civil Society in India." *LSE International Development Working Paper Series* 22-206 March.

10 Rajeshwari, B., Nandini Deo, and Margit van Wessel. 2020. "Negotiating Autonomy in Capacity Development: Addressing the Inherent Tension." *World Development* 134, 105046.

AFTER CORPORATE SOCIAL RESPONSIBILITY 137

as nonprofit board members have shifted the internal management of many CSOs. It has made them more cautious, less likely to engage in political advocacy, and more oriented toward shorter-term interventions that lend themselves to impact assessment. This is the corporatization of civil society professionals. The blurring of boundaries between a career in making profits for corporations and in building relationships with communities to resist the harms caused by runaway corporate growth is a loss for a healthy society.

The corporatization of civil society organizations, agendas, ideology, and people is the most meaningful change that has come from the past decade of CSR in India. While it has led to greater transparency and a new focus on measuring impact, these gains do not outweigh the gravity of the loss. It has been a decade of impoverishing democratic discourse and a loss of imagination for alternative paths to inclusive and sustainable development. While India has been remarkably successful at reducing levels of absolute extreme poverty in the past few years, as discussed in Chapter 3, the social divisions and polarization of society are increasing.[11] The electoral dominance of the BJP makes more attention to inclusivity highly unlikely. This also means that the coalition between the government and its preferred corporations can grow stronger and deeper.[12]

For neoliberal, or liberal Skeptics who argue that corporations do not have any obligations to society beyond their own pursuit of economic profit, this book may provide support for their belief that corporations should not try to do good. After all, I am arguing that the corporate form is unsuited to pursue projects of sustainability and inclusivity. The point of departure between those Skeptics and myself is simply that I think that because of their impersonal and insatiable greed, corporations need to be regulated. The economic sphere of our lives can and must be brought under the regulation of our democratic institutions and impulses. Through workplace democracies, state regulation, and other more creative responses, the harmful effects of corporate wealth creation must be tamed. This will come at a cost to us all in terms of the goods and services we consume. Some of them will cease to be produced, and others modified in design or quantity. But the payoff is that we will be making

---

11 Sahoo, Niranjan. 2020. "Mounting Majoritarianism and Political Polarization in India," in Thomas Carothurs and Andrew O'Donahue (Eds.). *Political Polarization in South and Southeast Asia*. Washington, DC: Carnegie Endowment for International Peace.

12 Jayant, Pankaj and Shivan Mogha. 2021. "The corporate-government nexus in Indian politics." *Polis Project*. New York, NY. November 25. Available at https://www.thepolisproject.com/read/the-corporate-government-nexus-in-indian-politics-an-analysis-of-corporate-backed-electoral-trusts/ (accessed December 2023).

138   CORPORATE SOCIAL RESPONSIBILITY AND CIVIL SOCIETY

collective and intentional choices about how to use our shared resources of time, attention, and things.

CSR, Philanthropy, Democracy, or [...]?

This book has shown that CSR collaborations with CSOs by themselves are not going to produce the innovations in practice and policy needed to put India on a path to sustainable and inclusive development. This section considers the alternatives. Can philanthropy by the wealthy serve as a catalyst for social and economic change? While most observers have argued they cannot, I add a brief consideration of the neuroscience literature that helps explain why they cannot. Most of those who reject philanthropy as a path to solving society's ills argue that the state under democratic control is the best instrument to create a more just economy and culture. While I am sympathetic to this argument, I also take seriously the critiques of democracy operating within the nation-state system.[13] Therefore, I am not sure that our democratic institutions are able to achieve sustainable and inclusive development either. This leaves us with few options. I suppose one could always withdraw from the capitalist economy and nation-state into small enclaves of resistance—the hermit option.[14] This feels inadequate as it is only self-oriented and I don't say more about this alternative. Or one could engage in an imaginative and creative project that experiments with alternative ways of being until one of these experiments grows attractive enough to others to adopt. There are some people engaged in these utopian experiments and I end the book by suggesting we study them more closely as we continue to search for a more sustainable and inclusive world.

The Rich Are Rentiers—One fascinating study provides neuroscientific evidence to support other work showing that class and empathy are related.[15] People with fewer resources show heightened prefrontal cortex responses to images of others in pain than rich people. Poor people are better at identifying that another person is in pain.[16] Other studies show that there is a strong

---

13 Roy, Arundhati. 2009. *Fieldnotes on Democracy*. Chicago: Haymarket Books; Brown, Wendy. 2023. *Nihilistic Times*. Cambridge, MA: Harvard University Press.

14 Smith-Cavros, Eileen and Arianna Sunyak. 2018. "Off-the-Grid in an On-Grid Nation: Household Energy Choices, Intra-Community Effects, and Attitudes in a Rural Neighborhood in Utah." *Journal of Ecological Anthropology*. 20(1). https://digitalcommons.usf.edu/cgi/viewcontent.cgi?article=1214&context=jea (accessed December 2, 2023).

15 Varnum, Michael E. W., Chris Blais, Ryan S. Hampton, and Gene A. Brewer. 2015. "Social Class Affects Neural Empathic Responses." *Culture and Brain*. 3, 122–133.

16 Kraus, M. W., S. Coˆte´, and D. Keltner. 2010. "Social Class, Contextualism, and Empathic Accuracy." *Psychological Science*. 21, 1716–1723.

AFTER CORPORATE SOCIAL RESPONSIBILITY

relationship between class and ethical behavior, which suggests that we should not rely on the wealthy to act as trustees because they are far too comfortable with lying, cheating, and harming others to benefit themselves. A meta-study gathered data from seven studies to show that wealthier people engage in more cheating, lying, and aggression toward others. They suggest that the greater access to wealth and therefore independence of the rich make them more greedy and this lets them justify more unethical behavior.[17] This tendency is the flip side of the generosity of the poor. Research suggests that people with fewer resources engage in more prosocial behavior than the wealthy because they are dependent on others. Their empathy is connected to their lives, which are lived with the support of others in a way that is not true of the wealthy.[18] The bottom line is that the wealthy can be thought of as rentiers—people who profit off their ownership of assets, rather than producing anything useful. They are skilled at profiting from renting their often inherited assets to the needy, not at solving problems, mobilizing resources for the greater good, or creating new value. Relying on rentiers to solve difficult social problems is a fool's errand.

This rentier literature studies the relationship between inequality and philanthropy. It builds on the insight that the rich are truly different in how they understand their responsibilities to others who are suffering. There is mixed evidence on whether higher levels of inequality make the wealthy more generous or less. Some authors suggest there is no relationship between inequality and the level of giving by the wealthy.[19] Further, studies of family owned businesses (which dominate India's economy) show that they behave in ways that fail to even maximize profit in favor of preserving family ownership over the well-being of the employees or other stakeholders of

---

17 Piff, Paul K., Daniel M. Stancato, Stéphane Côté, Rodolfo Mendoza-Denton, and Dacher Keltner. 2012. "Higher Social Class Predicts Increased Unethical Behavior." *Proceedings of the National Academy of Sciences of the USA.* 109(11), 4086–4091.

18 Robinson, Angela R. and Paul K. Piff. 2017. "Deprived, but Not Depraved: Prosocial Behavior Is an Adaptive Response to Lower Socioeconomic Status." *Behavioral and Brain Sciences.* 40. Available at doi: 10.1017/S0140525X17001108 (accessed March 12, 2024).

19 Côté, S., J. House, and R. Willer. 2015. "High Economic Inequality Leads Higher-Income Individuals to Be Less Generous." *Proceedings of the National Academy of Sciences of the USA.* 112(52), 15838–15843; Suss, J. 2023. "Higher Income Individuals Are More Generous When Local Economic Inequality Is High." *PLoS One.* 18(6). Available at https://doi.org/10.1371/journal.pone.0286273 (accessed March 9, 2024); Schmukle, S. C., M. Korndörfer, and B. Egloff. 2019. "No Evidence that Economic Inequality Moderates the Effect of Income on Generosity." *Proceedings of the National Academy of Sciences of the USA.* 116(20), 9790–9795.

the company. Building on findings that family owned firms often engage in behavior that looks irrational from a purely profit orientation, some scholars show that over time, in response to context, family firm owners can shift their perspectives. As these perspectives shift due to socialization into a different set of goals and values, these firms adopt new strategies showing the variation among family owned firms over time.[20] In contrast to socio-emotional wealth perspectives on family firms that emphasize the nonfinancial aspects of business ownership, the rentier perspective focuses on how these family firms manage generational wealth.[21] Ultimately, the rich behave differently than the rest of us. They prioritize their own interests, narrowly defined, over those of their workers, customers, and fellow citizens. The wealthy will not, cannot, support sustainable and inclusive development.

Philanthropy can be worse than simply ineffective. It can become the means by which to hollow out democracy. As Giridharadas explains, "When a society helps people through its shared democratic institutions, it does so on behalf of all, and in a context of equality. Those institutions, representing those free and equal citizens, are making a collective choice of whom to help and how. Those who receive help are not only objects of a transaction, but also subjects of it—citizens with agency."[22] Critics of technocratic approaches to sustainable and inclusive development agree that "Effective democracy is the antidote to the tyranny of foreign [or corporate] good intentions."[23] Some argue that the least worst option is strengthening the state and trusting democracy politics.[24] This faith in democratic politics sounds logical but the evidence of the past decade should make us all cautious of relying on electoral democracy to be able to liberate us. After all, electoral democracy is operating within global capitalism and the nation-state system. Both of these ways of organizing our economies and politics throw up limits on what democratic governments can achieve. Corporate media, xenophobic

---

20 Nason, R., A. Mazzelli, and M. Carney. 2019a. "The Ties that Unbind: Socialization and Business-Owning Family Reference Point Shift." *Academy of Management Review.* 44(4), 846–870.

21 Nason, Robert S., Michael Carney, Isabelle Le Breton-Miller, and Danny Miller. 2019b. "Who Cares about Socioemotional Wealth? SEW and Rentier Perspectives on the One Percent Wealthiest Business Households." *Journal of Family Business Strategy.* 10(2), 144–158.

22 Giridharadas, Anand. 2108. *Winners Take All: The Elite Charade of Changing the World.* New York, NY: Knopf.

23 Deaton, Angus. 2013. *The Great Escape: Health, Wealth, and the Origins of Inequality.* Princeton, NJ: Princeton University Press.

24 Rieff, David. 2015. *The Reproach of Hunger: Food, Justice, and Money in the Twenty-First Century.* New York, NY: Simon & Schuster.

AFTER CORPORATE SOCIAL RESPONSIBILITY   141

nationalism, and the global financial system shift the attention of most people away from the truly powerful and make scapegoats out of the most vulnerable. Instead of eating the rich, people vote to exclude refugees and punish the socially marginal. Looking at the popular support for leaders like Victor Orban, Narendra Modi, Donald Trump, Vladimir Putin, Jair Bolsanaro, and others, one may reasonably wonder if democracy's days are done. Majoritarianism and mobilization seem to be outweighing projects of mutual support. But if democracy isn't the solution, what is?

The truth is that I don't have any clear solutions to the challenge before us. I do know that there are utopian experiments unfolding around the world that are seeking alternative pathways to justice and equity. One of the best-known spaces for imagining alternatives to neoliberalism are the gatherings held at the World Social Forum. These began in 2001 in the wake of the massive protests against the IMF and World Bank in Seattle and have become an annual space for dissidents and social movements to connect. The first two WSF were held in the city of Porto Alegro, Brazil, which itself is trying a radically democratic and solidarity-based governance model. Porto Alegro's example of self-sufficiency and the discussions and reflections after the WSF are one of the spaces in which alternative futures for the planet are being created.[25] While there have been tensions between the elite who provided the initial networks and organization for the WSF and the grassroots activists who provide it with credibility and do the hard organizing work with marginalized communities, they overcame them sufficiently for the gatherings to continue.[26] The upcoming gathering in Nepal proclaims, "In fact, humanity is on the brink of multi-faceted calamities leading to the destruction of its own survival. Given the threat is real and urgent, the ideals of the new world order that rests upon sustainability, dignity, co-existence, equality, and equity must be enacted and actualized. With the pledge of 'Another world is possible' the World Social Forum (WSF) emerges as a beacon of hope, more essential than ever before."[27] However, in recent years, frustration has grown that the WSF hasn't evolved beyond its original mandate of providing a space for discussion. Some have called for it to actually try to shape global politics and many have simply stopped attending, choosing to place their energy

---

25 Teivainen, T. 2002. The World Social Forum and Global Democratisation: Learning from Porto Alegre. *Third World Quarterly*. 23(4), 621–632.

26 Pleyers, 2009. "The World Social Forum, a Globalisation from Below?" *Societies without Borders*. 3(1), 71–89.

27 World Social Forum Nepal. 2023. Available at https://www.wsf2024nepal.org/aboutOrganization (accessed December 2023).

142 CORPORATE SOCIAL RESPONSIBILITY AND CIVIL SOCIETY

in other initiatives.[28] Mobilization and persistence are always harder for insurgents than those in power.

An even more decentralized and fragmented arena in which people are experimenting with other futures is the world of homeschooling (or home-educating) families. It is difficult to get an exact headcount of families voluntarily choosing to keep their children out of formal schools. In some countries, this practice is illegal, while in about two-thirds of the world, it is permitted, albeit with varying levels of regulation and supervision.[29] In conducting the research for this book, I traveled to India on multiple occasions with my children, with longer stays in 2019 and 2023. During the longer visits, I reached out to homeschooling networks here and came across a subculture of people engaged in self-directed education. Unlike the stereotypical religious fundamentalists who want to control their children, these families are experimenting with ways of empowering children to be the authors of their own lives. In learning communities like Sadhana in Mumbai, Arohi in Karnataka, and the Shikshantar Andolan in Udaipur, families gather using the principles of the gift economy and collectively create learning spaces for their children. They are experimenting with how education can be a pathway to liberation. And most of them quickly discover that in this journey the parents end up changing the most.

In the US, public schools are often seen as a critical public good that is both a product of democracy and a requisite for it. Schools teach shared languages and histories, thus contributing to nation-building.[30] They should serve a diverse range of families and offer equality of opportunity to all children. Recent research points to public school as an important institution for managing conflict and indoctrinating marginal populations into state-building projects.[31] Critics of private schools have often pointed out

---

28 Savio, Robert. 2022. "The demise of the WSF," January 26. Available at https://www.meer.com/en/68425-the-demise-of-the-world-social-forum (accessed December 2023).

29 Yin, D. 2022. "The Importance and Relevance of Home Education: Global Trends and Insights from the United States." Paper commissioned as part of the GEM Report Fellowship Programme in 2022. UNESCO; Ray, B. D. 2021. "An Overview of the Worldwide Rise and Expansion of Home Education Homeschooling." in R. English (Ed.). *Global Perspectives on Home Education in the 21st Century* (pp. 1–18). IGI Global.

30 Darden, K. and H. Mylonas. 2016. "Threats to Territorial Integrity, National Mass Schooling, and Linguistic Commonality." *Comparative Political Studies.* 49(11), 1446–1479.

31 Paglayan, A. 2022. "Education or Indoctrination? The Violent Origins of Public School Systems in an Era of State-Building." *American Political Science Review.* 116, 4.

AFTER CORPORATE SOCIAL RESPONSIBILITY

that withdrawing from public school systems in the US was motivated by racial animus in the wake of *Brown v. BOE*[32] and that today's private school families are engaged in opportunity hoarding.[33] Another form of withdrawal from public education is through homeschooling, which can be a way to meet the needs of individual students for a bespoke education[34] and also a way for parents to control what their children are exposed to in terms of secular and diverse ideas, even amounting to child abuse (Bartholet 2019).[35] A subset of homeschooling families have adopted unschooling as their approach to education. Unschooling is a form of child-directed education in which parents act as facilitators while children's interests and passions guide the learning. This form of homeschooling calls for parents to actively cede their power over their children and instead act as fiduciaries who constantly seek ways to empower the child. The promise of this path is not a well-groomed and socially networked student as offered by private schools. Neither is it someone socialized into the norms of contemporary society.[36] So why do it? In the context of decolonization, a number of families in the majority world and some who are members of marginalized groups within the Global North are adopting unschooling as a way to live out their radical, feminist, egalitarian, and decolonial political visions.[37] They are living their political ideals by actively learning to live as equals with their children. By respecting the most powerless in society (children), they are practicing what it would look like to have a social order based on equality, nurture, mutual respect, and a rejection of capitalist materialism.

The World Social Forum and the thousands of families that are part of the self-directed education movement are very different arenas in which experiments with imagining, creating, and living a different kind of future are unfolding. Unlike corporations trying to balance the impact of their production processes, their promotion of materialistic consumerism, and their glorification of unsustainable lifestyles with a little philanthropy on

---

32 Southern Education Foundation. 2016. "A History of Private Schools and Race." Available at https://southerneducation.org/publications/history-of-private-schools-and-race-in-the-american-south/ (accessed December 2023).

33 Sattin-Bajaj, C. and A. Roda. 2020. "Opportunity Hoarding in School Choice Contexts: The Role of Policy Design in Promoting Middle-Class Parents' Exclusionary Behaviors." *Educational Policy*. 34(7), 992–1035.

34 Martin, J. 2023. "What is homeschooling?" *Parents*, July 5.

35 Bartholet, Elizabeth. 2020. "Homeschooling: Parent Rights Absolutism vs Child Rights to Education and Protection." *Arizona Law Review*. 62, 1.

36 Alliance for Self Directed Education. 2023. https://www.self-directed.org/ (accessed December 1, 2023).

37 Richard, Akilah. 2020. *Raising Free People*. Binghamton, NY: PM Press.

the side, these networks are making the reimagination of inclusivity and sustainability their central work. Many of them, probably most of them, are following pathways that will lead to dead ends or that fail to inspire anyone beyond their own narrow circle. But what if some of them stumble onto ways of living a more inclusive, sustainable, and joyful life? Finding out how to listen to them, and how to learn from them, is an exciting possibility and direction for future research.

INDEX

aam admi 56, 57
Aditya Birla Group 37
Ahluwalia, Montek Singh 57
Akshaya Patra 2, 109, 110, 112
Ambani, Mukesh 1
Ambedkar, B. R. 44, 75, 76
Ashoka University 106

Birla, Ritu 13, 14
brain drain 18
bureaucracy 30, 53, 56, 62–65, 103, 123

capitalism 11, 28, 37, 47, 64, 80, 85, 89, 124, 132, 134, 140
Citizens United 25
Coca-Cola 35, 93–97, 108
colonialism 22, 42, 80
Companies Act 15, 25, 58, 63, 91, 92, 113, 115, 117, 133
consultants 116, 129, 130

Dalit 46, 60, 77, 79
democracy 1, 25, 26, 29, 30, 32, 47, 125, 132, 134, 138, 140–42
depoliticization 14, 32

East India Company 21–23
efficiency 11, 31, 34, 36, 63, 66, 82, 95, 100, 109–11, 113, 136

FCRA 26, 48–52
Friedman, Milton 24

Gandhi, Indira 46, 50
Gandhi, M. K. 37, 38, 45, 81
Gandhi, Rajiv 47, 83
Gandhi, Sonia 48
Gandhian trusteeship model 37

gender 39, 44, 71, 73–76, 78, 79, 84, 89, 136
German foreign aid 58, 59
Giridharadas, Anand 2, 6, 140
greenwashing 12, 39

Hindu code 45
Hindutva 31, 52, 53, 124, 133, 134

ideological corporatization 132, 136
impact assessment 12, 106, 117, 118, 121, 124, 135, 137
inclusive development 6, 8, 9, 14, 16, 18, 19, 37, 70, 89, 90, 113, 115, 138, 140
Intelligence Bureau 51
International Poverty Line 72

land reforms 45
liberalization 48, 63, 64, 82, 84

majoritarianism 137, 141
materialism 29, 32, 143
middle path 16, 17
MNREGA 48
Modi, Narendra 141
Modi government 51–53, 124
Multidimensional Poverty Index 72

National Advisory Council 48, 49
Nehru, Jawaharlal 44, 81
neoliberalism 56, 57, 65, 124, 141
neuroscience 138
Nihilists 2, 8, 11, 12, 16–18, 133, 134
Niti Ayog 53, 127

pinkwashing 12, 39
public sector enterprises 23, 25, 41, 44, 62, 64, 81, 127

Reliance Industries 93
Rentiers 138
Roy, Arundhati 2, 6, 57, 132, 138

savarna 65, 66
Skeptics 2, 137
Soviet Union 45, 47
sustainable development 1, 2, 5, 8, 10, 17, 18, 51, 54, 69, 85, 87, 90, 94, 108, 131, 134, 136, 137

Tata, Ratan 61
Tata Group 37, 38
Tata Institute of Social Sciences 106
Tata Motors 93
Trusteeship 37, 38

United Progressive Alliance 49–51, 60

Wada Na Todo Abhiyan 48
World Social Forum 141, 143

Printed in the USA
CPSIA information can be obtained
at www.ICGtesting.com
JSHW021205100824
67866JS00001B/2